WHAT THE CRITICS ARE SAYING ABOUT THIS BOOK

"If your life is meaningless, let me TURN YOU ON to this book."

— D. Lopez, *La Prensa*, San Diego

"*The Golden Door to Retirement and Living*, is ESSENTIAL reading for those thinking of living in Costa Rica."

—*Costa Rica Today*

"You'll get all the insiders' low down from this GREAT book."

—Dianne Bartely, *The Nashville Tennessean*

"Potential residents of Costa Rica, shouldn't leave home WITHOUT this book."

—*Dallas Morning News*

"*The Golden Door to Retirement and Living in Costa Rica* offers LOADS of USEFUL information for the permanent resident."

—Jack Reber, *The San Diego-Tribune*

"This book offers HELPFUL advice to any would-be resident of Costa Rica."

—Mary Ellen Botter, Travel Editor, *Denver Post*

"This book is PACKED with PRACTICAL information for both retirees and tourists who want an entree to the local scene."

—*Chicago Tribune*

"Retire in Costa Rica...*The Golden Door to Retirement and Living in Costa Rica* tells HOW."

—Thomas Ropp, *The Arizona Republic*

"It's FULL of VALUABLE information, paints a CLEAR picture of what life is like for foreigners living there and is very DOWN-TO-EARTH."

—*Travel Writer Marketletter*

"It is a guide to the GOOD LIFE and contains EVERYTHING you need to know."

—*The Edmonton Sun Travel Digest*

THE GOLDEN DOOR TO RETIREMENT AND LIVING IN COSTA RICA

A guide to inexpensive living in a peaceful tropical paradise

Written by
CHRISTOPHER HOWARD

In collaboration with
LAMBERT JAMES

iii

THE GOLDEN DOOR TO RETIREMENT AND LIVING IN COSTA RICA

By Christopher Howard
With Lambert James

Illustrator: G. Garcia

Seventh Edition

First Edition, published in Costa Rica
Second through Seventh Editions
Published in United States

© 1995-6 M.G. Robinson

ISBN 1-881233-30-8

Costa Rica Books
P.O. Box 1512
Thousand Oaks, CA 91358

If there be any splendor in peace, let it rest in a country like this. . .

The authors

ACKNOWLDGEMENTS

This edition would not have become a reality without the invaluable help of many people.

I would first like to thank my typesetter, Debbie Murray, for her hard work and patience.

I am also very grateful to Shirley Miller, the publisher of the *Costa Rican Outlook*, for her inspiration and guidance during all stages of the development of this latest edition.

A special thanks to Ellen Searby, author of the best-selling *Costa Rica Traveler*, for giving me the knowledge to open some important doors that have helped my career immensely.

I would also like to thank Anne Becher, Robert Grey and the rest of the staff at Publications in English for believing in me and helping promote my book in Costa Rica.

I am indebted to all the critics whose many favorable reviews made my last edition a success.

I would like to acknowledge all of the help I have received from the Publishers Marketing Association's book promotional programs. Thanks to them, this book is now being sold in most major bookstores in the U.S. and Canada.

Also, I am appreciative of the help the *Costa Rica Today* and *Tico Times* have given me with my advertising campaign.

Finally, I would like to express my eternal gratitude to members of my family for their constant support when I needed it the most.

Chris Howard
San José, Costa Rica

ABOUT THE AUTHORS

The author, Christopher Howard and his collaborator, Lambert James, are fluent Spanish-speaking retirees who together have lived in Costa Rica for over twenty years.

During that time they have had the opportunity to gather a great amount of accurate information related to retirement and living in Costa Rica. Therefore, it is not surprising that they have first-hand knowledge and insight into all aspects of Costa Rica's culture, its people and its government.

This book is based on painstaking research on a variety of related subjects and is the culmination of their collective efforts.

Chris Howard has an extensive foreign language background having earned a B.A. in Spanish and Latin American studies from the University of California at Los Angeles, and a Master's degree in Spanish from the University of California. He also has a teaching credential to teach Spanish at all levels from California State University, San Francisco.

In addition, he was the recipient of scholarships for graduate study at the University of the Americas in Puebla, Mexico and the Jesuit University of Guadalajara, Mexico.

He written two foreign language books and help start a language institute in San José, Costa Rica.

Currently, he is compiling information for a book about Costa Rican idioms, his specialty, and writing a highly acclaimed weekly newspaper column for one of Costa Rica's English language newspapers. He is also working on a movie script about Costa Rica.

TABLE OF CONTENTS

CHAPTER X

FOREWORD

This all-encompassing book is the most complete work available on retirement and living in beautiful Costa Rica. It is intended to orient and familiarize everyone, not just those who are ready to retire, with the "Little Switzerland of America"—Costa Rica. This book is designed to guide people of all ages seeking to change their lives by moving to a new and exotic land outside of the United States.

Reading this easy-to-understand guidebook will help save you time, money and hassles. You will learn how to live and survive in Costa Rica from all of the insider information and thousands of valuable tips we have included.

Use our book for reference while you live in comfort for less than you ever dreamed possible. Many Americans living below the poverty level in the United States can live in moderate luxury on a modest retirement income in Costa Rica.

They can enjoy one of the best year-round climates in the world (72 degree average in the Central Valley) and live with the generally polite Costa Rican people, who actually like Americans. The U.S. system and culture are admired and often imitated and English is virtually the second language.

All this only two and one-half hours by air from the United States via Miami and even accessible by car.

Costa Rica is a tranquil, safe and relatively crime-free country. Because of this peaceful atmosphere, many compare it to the United States of 30 years ago, when life was unhurried, unspoiled, and uncrowded. Costa Rica is also the healthiest country south of Canada and has a higher life-expectancy rate than the United States.

All things considered, Costa Rica is one of the best places on earth to live because of the excellent quality of life.

Inexpensive medical care, affordable housing, excellent transportation and communication's network, tax incentives, every imaginable activity to stay busy, a government that goes to great lengths to make retirement as easy as possible

TYPICAL OXCART OR *CARRETA*

and encourages investment, combine to make Costa Rica tops on the list of retirement havens.

According to a survey of potential foreign retirement areas in the *Robb Report,* Costa Rica surpasses all countries including Mexico, Puerto Rico, Spain, Portugal, Australia, the Caribbean Islands and Greece.

No wonder there are more Canadians and Americans living in Costa Rica than any other country in Latin America—an estimated 25,000 full-time residents— two thousand of of whom are official retirees or *pensionados.*

In short, this beautiful country has the warmth and flavor of Mexico, without the anti-Americanism, the physical beauty of Guatemala without a large military presence, the sophistication of Brazil without abject proverty or violent crime and more winter sunshine than Hawaii or Florida and less people to share it with.

It's not too late to join others for what living was made for...PLEASURE. Enjoy this book and thank you for considering and selecting Costa Rica as your place to live. We hope you will find this book interesting, and an impetus to discovering new things, as we open the "GOLDEN DOOR" to the best of retirement and living, on a budget everyone can afford NOW!

INTRODUCTION

WELCOME TO BEAUTIFUL COSTA RICA

Costa Rica's friendly three million people, or *Ticos* as they call themselves, invite you to come and experience their tranquil country, with its long and beautiful coastlines, alluring waters of the Caribbean and the Pacific, pristine beaches and some of the most picturesque surroundings you have ever laid your eyes on. Many visitors say Costa Rica is even more beautiful than Hawaii, and best of all is still unspoiled. Costa Rica has Hawaii's weather without the high prices and offers more beauty and adventure per acre than any other place in the world.

In the heart of the Central Valley, surrounded by beautiful rolling mountains and volcanoes, sits San José, today's capital and largest city in the country. Viewed from above, this area looks like some parts of Switzerland.

San José has a mixture of modern and colonial architecture yet remains charmingly quaint despite being a fairly large city with a slightly cosmopolitan flavor. Even though the San José area has a population of over one million people, you always get a small-town feeling, due to the layout of the city.

San José or *Chepe*, as the locals call it, is also the cultural center of the country. It offers good shopping, varied night life, a wide range of hotels, art galleries, theatres, museums, two English newspapers and much more.

Finally, because of San José's convenient location any part of the country is accessible in a matter of hours by automobile. We recommend that you use San José as a starting point or home base while you explore Costa Rica and look for a permanent place to reside.

CHAPTER ONE

Costa Rica's Land, History and People

COSTA RICA

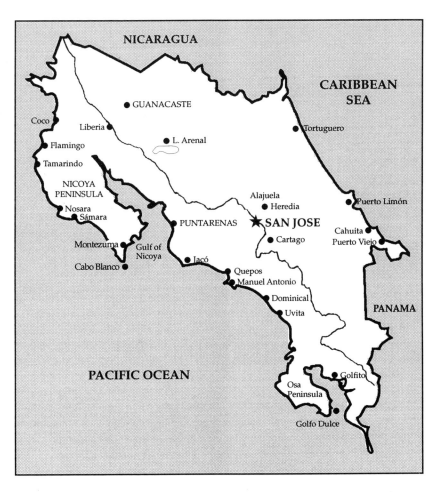

NICARAGUA

CARIBBEAN SEA

● GUANACASTE

Coco

Liberia ●

Flamingo

Tamarindo

NICOYA PENINSULA

Nosara

Sámara

Montezuma ●

Cabo Blanco ●

Gulf of Nicoya

● L. Arenal

PUNTARENAS

● Jacó

Alajuela

● Heredia

★ SAN JOSE

● Cartago

Quepos

Manuel Antonio

Dominical

Uvita

● Tortuguero

● Puerto Limón

Cahuita ●

Puerto Viejo ●

PANAMA

PACIFIC OCEAN

Osa Peninsula

Golfito

Golfo Dulce

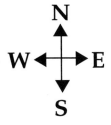

N

W ◀ ▶ E

S

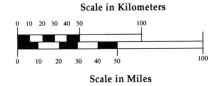

—— Pan American Highway

Scale in Kilometers

0 10 20 30 40 50   100

0   10   20   30   40   50   100

Scale in Miles

GEOGRAPHY

Costa Rica occupies a territory of around 20,000 square miles (about the size of the state of West Virginia) in the southern part of Central America, and includes several small islands mostly on the Pacific side. It is much like the state of Florida with it's two long coastlines. The country is only about 200 miles long and 70 miles wide at the narrowest part.

Costa Rica's three mountain ranges create five geographically diverse areas. The Northern Central Plains, the Northwest Peninsula, the Tropical Lowlands on the Pacific and Caribbean coasts and the Central Valley where 70 percent of the population resides.

Costa Rica is often compared to Switzerland and Hawaii because of its mountains and forests. Unlike many areas of Mexico, Central and South America it remains beautiful and warm year-round. This is partly because it borders the Pacific Ocean on the west, the Atlantic Ocean on the east, and has a string of towering volcanoes on the

Central Plateau. Combine all this and you have a unique tropical paradise.

Lastly, Costa Rica is divided into seven beautiful but geographically different provinces: Alajuela, Cartago, Guanacaste, Heredia, Puntarenas, Limón and San José.

WEATHER

In Costa Rica you will dress on the lighter side year-round and enjoy one of the best climates in the world. Temperatures vary little from season to season and fluctuate with altitude. The higher you go the colder it gets, and the lower you go the warmer it is. In the Central Plateau spring-like daytime temperatures hover around 72 degrees all year, while lower elevations enjoy temperatures ranging from the upper 70s to the high 80s. Temperatures at sea level fluctuate between the high 80s and low 90s in summer with slightly more humidity than at higher elevations.

Like other tropical places, Costa Rica only has two seasons. The summer or *verano* is generally from late December to April with March and April being the warmest months of the year. The rainy season or *invierno*, runs from May to November. January is usually the coolest month. At times, there is an unseasonal dry spell or Indian summer in either July, August or September. The Costa Ricans call this pause in the rainy weather, *veranillo*.

Unlike many of the world's tropical areas, during the wet season almost all mornings are sunny and clear with only a few hours of rain in the afternoons. Since the temperature varies little, the wet months are usually as warm as the dry months. It is unusual to have two or three days of continuous rainy weather in most areas of the country. October is usually the rainiest month of the year.

However, the Caribbean Coast tends to be wet all year long. For this reason many foreigners choose to live on the West Coast of Costa Rica. This climate, along with a unique geography, is responsible for Costa Rica's lush vegetation and greenness at all elevations especially during the rainy season.

WHERE TO LIVE IN COSTA RICA

Since we have just discussed Costa Rica's geography and weather, now is a good time to talk about some of the things to consider before choosing a permanent place to live.

Deciding where to live in Costa Rica depends on your preferences. If you like the stimulation of urban living and spring-like weather all year, you will probably be happiest living in **San José** or one of the adjacent smaller towns and cities in the Central Valley. As we mention later in this book there is a plethora of activities for a retiree in, around and near San José. Retirement is a big change for many people because they find themselves with more free time than usual and sometimes get bored. This should not occur if you reside in the San José area because there is a large North American colony and it is always easy to find something to do.

If you don't want to live far from town, many Americans live in the fashionable suburb of **Rohrmoser,** on the west-side of Sabana Park. This area has many beautiful homes of wealthy Costa Ricans and is considered very safe since a large number of well-guarded foreign embassies are there. A few supermarkets, good restaurants, and the Plaza Mayor Shopping Center are also in this area. The only thing bad about Rohrmoser is that bus service to downtown San José is not that good, but you can always take a taxi since cabs are so affordable.

About five minutes east of downtown San José, is the residential neighborhood of **Los Yoses.** Many foreigners live in this area, because it is only a short walk to downtown San José. The North American Cultural Center is here, so there are interesting activities to keep a person occupied. Los Yoses also boasts a bowling alley, a supermarket complex, a bookstore and many bars and restaurants.

Just east of Los Yoses is **San Pedro**—the home of the University of Costa Rica. The campus and surrounding area resemble many U.S. college towns, with its many sidewalk cafes, restaurants, bookstores, night-spots and boutiques. Some interesting event or cultural activity is always there. During April the annual University Week celebration takes place. This event includes floats and a carnival-like atmosphere.

Another place you might consider living is **Escazú**—a popular suburb where many Americans reside. Escazú is about five miles west of San José, 10 to 15 minutes driving time on the old two-lane road or new *autopista,* (highway). Escazú is one of the most popular places English speaking foreigners live. Bus service is excellent to and from San José. You can catch either a micro-bus or regular bus in the park behind the church in downtown Escazú.

Despite being quaint and country-like, Escazú has pharmacies, mini-malls, supermarkets, excellent private schools, first-class restaurants, trendy shops, doctors, dentists, a post office and much more. You don't have to go to San José unless you want to. There is also a beautiful private country club and golf course. Housing is plentiful, but expensive, because Escazú is popular with wealthy Costa Ricans, and well-to-do foreigners. However, if you are living on a budget or small pension you can find more affordable housing in San Antonio de Escazú. Finally, Escazú's American Legion Post is "the gathering place" for Americans to socialize, participate in many activities and make new friends and connections.

Santa Ana, in the Valley of the Sun, about four miles west of Escazú, is another good place to live. Many foreigners and Costa Ricans reside there. You can get to Santa Ana by taking the old scenic road from Escazú through the hills, or by the new highway. We recommend checking out this town. It is more rural and less developed than Escazú, but there are good supermarkets and some shopping. Lately there has been a building boom in the area. On the minus side, at times bus service can be slow to San José.

Cuidad Colón, located about twenty minutes beyond Santa Ana, is the farthest western suburb of San Jose. Some foreigners live there.

La Garita, a pleasant area west of the airport on the road to Quepos, is said to have one of the best climates in Costa Rica. There are many foreigners living in this town. Some large homes come with large parcels of land. We have a friend who rented a home with a pool, a couple of acres of land and a watchman for a very reasonable price. There is also a small zoo and an excellent restaurant called La Fiesta del Maíz in La Garita. The town of **San Antonio de Belén**, behind the airport and just a couple of miles off the main highway, is also a good place to live. The Ojo de Agua recreational complex is in this area.

If you wish to combine an urban life and warmer weather, you can reside in San José's neighboring city **Alajuela**, which is also near the airport. This city is about 20 minutes by bus from downtown San José and has everything you want in a city without the city feeling. The bus service is excellent during the day, so it is easy to commute to San José if necessary. Because of the warm climate many Americans live in Alajuela, so you can easily make new acquaintances. There are nice parks, movies, doctors, supermarkets and more in this

COSTA RICA'S LAND, HISTORY AND PEOPLE

city, so it is not necessary to go to San José often. Housing is also very reasonably priced and plentiful.

Heredia, halfway between San José and Alajuela at the foot of Poás Volcano, is also a nice city. It is only a short distance from San José by car or bus. Not as many foreign retirees live in Heredia as in Alajuela, but it is still a good place to live. The surrounding countryside is very beautiful, especially above the city. Heredia also has a university.

San Rafael de Heredia is in the hills above the city of Heredia. The most notable feature of this area is the climate, which is considerably cooler than that in San José. Wealthy Costa Ricans and some foreigners live there.

Another neighboring city, **Cartago**, "just over the hill" from San José, is not as conveniently located because of the terrain. Perhaps because of the cooler year-round temperatures, fewer North Americans reside there. Bus service from San José to downtown Cartago is excellent because many Costa Ricans living in Cartago work in San José. The nicest thing about Cartago is its proximity to the beautiful **Orosi Valley**. Viewed from above, this valley is breathtaking. On the floor of the valley is a large man-made lake, **Cachí**, and a park where one can participate in many recreational activities from picnicking to water sports. The lake is fed by the famous **Reventazón** white-water river, that runs through the Orosi Valley.

If you prefer living in a cooler alpine-like setting, you can find nice homes and cabins all over the pine tree-covered mountains surrounding the Central Valley. Look at the areas around **Monte de La Cruz** and **San José de La Montaña**.

For those seeking a more relaxed life style, many other small towns and *fincas* (farms) are scattered all over the Central Valley. These places are ideal for people who can do without the excitement found in and around large cities.

Zarcero is a quaint little town famous for the sculptured bushes in front of its church. **San Ramón** is another tranquil town just off the main highway between San José and the port of Puntarenas on the Pacific Coast. **Grecia**, known as the cleanest town in Costa Rica, is also a place worth investigating.

Ciudad Quesada, more commonly known as San Carlos, is north of Grecia. We know a few North Americans who own ranches in this area. Almost everything of importance is found within several blocks of the town's main square.

Northwest of San Carlos is beautiful man-made **Lake Arenal.** This area is fast becoming popular with foreign residents. The Arenal volcano can often be seen smoking in the distance. Lake Arenal has excellent fishing, sailing, windsurfing and other outdoor activities. There is even a hot spring and resort located in nearby **Tabacón.**

If you are a beach enthusiast or warm weather person you have chosen the right country. As you will see in the section on beaches, (Chapter 4), Costa Rica has hundreds of miles of beautiful beaches to chose from.

The Caribbean coast, below **Puerto Limón**, has many places to live. This area particularly appeals to young people who like beautiful tropical settings, surfing and reggea music. A large colony of foreigners from Europe and the United States living in this area.

The village of **Cahuita**, probably the most popular spot on the Atlantic coast, lies next to Cahuita National Park and has one of the best beaches in the world. **Puerto Viejo**, a few miles to the south, is a great area for lovers of the Caribbean lifestyle with its snorkeling and surfing.

About nine kilometers down a dirt road are **Punta Uva**, with a gorgeous beach for swimming, and the fishing village of **Manzanillo**. This area is spectacular and undeveloped—but not for long.

The Caribbean coast sounds very enticing; however, the abundant year-round rainfall makes most Americans, Canadians and other foreigners choose to live on the drier west coast.

 Many breathtaking beaches all along the Pacific Coast in Guanacaste province are suitable for homes. However, many of the surrounding beach communities have too much tranquility for some people or resort atmosphere for others. **Playa del Coco** has an active night life and a small North American contingent living there to participate. **Tamarindo** also has a small foreign colony, but prices of property are very high. **Nosara** is an attractive area to live if you are a nature lover. An expatriate community flourishes there. **Montezuma**, a remote little fishing village near the tip of Nicoya Peninsula, has good beaches and attracts people interested in alternative lifestyles from all nations.

The central Pacific Coast also has some superb locations for living. This area has something for everyone—with swimming and surfing beaches, excellent sportfishing, as well as developed and undeveloped beaches and natural parks. If you like exuberant action, good waves and partying, we recommend **Jacó Beach**. However, be aware that Jacó is packed on most summer weekends, holidays and special occasions such as surf tournaments.

The **Quepos-Manuel Antonio** area is one of the most beautiful places in the world. Most foreigners live in and around the town of Quepos and along the road leading to **Manuel Antonio National Park**, a few kilometers south and over the hill.

Dominical, located 42 kilometers south of Quepos, is a less developed beach area which is developing quickly. Many expatriates are buying land and settling in the area.

In southern Costa Rica, some expatriates live around the port of **Golfito**, on the **Golfo Dulce Bay**. This drab, former banana town leaves a lot to be desired. However, there has been a lot of new development going on recently. Some Americans own large *fincas* (ranches, farms) and others live in more isolated areas around the gulf.

If you live in a beach or rural area, life is generally less expensive and more tranquil than in San José. If you live on a small budget, you might consider this factor before choosing a permanent place to settle.

In this section we have tried to give an idea of the more desirable places to live in Costa Rica. Since there are so many other great areas to choose from—it is impossible to describe all of them here—we suggest you read some of the guide books listed in the back of this book to get a better picture of what Costa Rica has to offer. Then you should plan to visit the places where you think you may want to live.

COSTA RICA'S UNIQUE HISTORY IN BRIEF

Traditionally Costa Rica has been a freedom-loving country living by democratic rules and respecting human rights.

When Columbus set foot on the Atlantic Coast at a place called Cariari (Puerto Limón) he anticipated finding vast amounts of gold, so he named this area COSTA RICA — "rich coast" in Spanish. However, unlike Mexico and Peru, Costa Rica had neither advanced Indian civilizations nor large deposits of gold. The small Indian population offered little resistance to the Spanish and was eventually wiped out by disease. Faced with no source of cheap labor, the Spanish colonists were forced to supply the labor themselves. Thus, a sort of democratic, equitable society developed with all doing their share of the work, and with few becoming very rich or very poor.

For a long time Costa Rica was almost forgotten by Spain, because she lacked trade and wealth. In fact, Costa Rica became so isolated and unimportant to the mother country that there was no War of Independence from Spain in the early 1800s, as there was in the rest of Latin America. Costa Ricans learned of their newly won independence from a letter which arrived one month after it was officially granted. This peaceful development continued well into the twentieth-century with only a few minor interruptions. The most notable feature of this process was the abolition of the army forever in 1948. The same year a new constitution was drafted that laid the groundwork for the most enduring democracy in Latin America.

The military has constantly threatened democratic institutions throughout the rest of turbulent Latin America. This is not the case in Costa Rica. Costa Rica has a 5,000-man, non-political national guard or police force under control of the civilian government. Like the police in the United States, they concentrate on enforcing the law and controlling traffic.

Because of a lack of large military expenditures that go with maintaining an army, Costa Rica has been able to establish one of the best all-encompassing Social Security systems in the world. It also developed an excellent public education system, hospitals, housing, modern communication systems and roads. As a result, Costa Rica has the largest proportion of middle class citizens in Latin America and a literacy rate of over ninety-percent. Furthermore, the prohibition of armed forces guarantees political stability and peace for future generations and reaffirms Costa Rica's dedication to a respect for human rights unequaled anywhere else in the world.

GOVERNMENT

Costa Rica's government has been an outstanding example of an enduring democracy for over forty years. Quite an achievement, when one looks at the rest of the world—particularly Latin America.

COSTA RICA'S FLAG

A neutral country, Costa Rica is compared to Switzerland because of its neutral political posture, with one exception; Costa Rica has no army. As we mentioned earlier, in 1948 Costa Ricans did what no other modern nation has done — they formally abolished their army. The same year they limited the power of their presidents, began universal suffrage and dedicated their government to justice and equality for all, thus ending discrimination and making Costa Rica a truly unique nation. Consequently, in Costa Rica you don't see any of the racial tension so prevalent in the United States and some other parts of the world. Non-citizens have the same rights as Costa Ricans. Today there is even a growing women's- rights movement.

Costa Ricans set up the legislative, judicial and executive power structure to prevent any one person or group from gaining too much power, and in order to ensure the continuity of the democratic process. For example, to eliminate the possibility of a dictatorship all presidents are limited to one term with **no** possibility of re-election. The members of the legislative assembly are also limited to a single four-year term and cannot be re-elected.

Costa Rica's two main political parties are the National Liberation Party and the United Social Christian Party.

Since Costa Rica is such a small country voters can participate more directly in the democratic process. Each vote carries more weight, so politicians are more accessible and have more contact with the people. Costa Ricans approach the presidential elections with such enthusiasm that they celebrate election day as if it were a big party or national holiday.

In Costa Rica people settle arguments at the ballot box, not on the battle field. A group of American Quakers established a colony because of this peaceful democratic tradition and the University of Peace was started and still exists near San José.

Finally, Costa Rica's former president, Dr. Oscar Arias Sánchez, was awarded the Nobel Peace Prize in 1987 for his efforts to spread peace and true democracy from Costa Rica to the rest of strife-torn Central America.

THE PEOPLE

Besides its excellent weather and natural beauty, Costa Rica's unique people are probably the country's most important resource and one of the main factors to consider in selecting Costa Rica as a place to live or retire.

Costa Ricans proudly call themselves *ticos.* This nickname derives from their habit of adding the ending *tico* to many words instead of *ito* as done in the rest of Central America.

Foreigners who have traveled in Mexico and other parts of Central America are quick to notice the racial and political differences between Costa Ricans and their neighbors .

Costa Ricans are mostly white and of Spanish origin with a mixture of German, Italian, English and other Europeans who have settled in Costa Rica over the years. This makes Costa Ricans the most racially homogeneous of all of the Central American people. Over 90% of the population is considered white or mestizo. Argentina and Uruguay are the only other countries in Latin America with similar racial compositions.

There is also a small black population of around 2%, mainly living on the Atlantic Coast, and a handful of Indians in the mountainous areas of the Central Plateau and along the Southeastern Coast. Costa Rica has never had a large Indian population like the other countries in the region.

Politically Costa Ricans have always been more democratic than their neighbors—especially during the last 30 years. Indeed they should be congratulated for being the only people to make democracy work in such a troubled region.

National Geographic reported several years ago that, when asked why Costa Rica isn't plagued by political instability and wars like her neighbors, a Costa Rican replied, in typical Costa Rican humor, or *vacilón*, "We are too busy making love and have no time for wars or revolutions."

Because they have the largest middle class of any of the Central American nations, Costa Ricans love to boast they have a classless society. Most people share the middle class mind set and tend to be more upwardly mobile than in other countries in the region. Although there is some poverty, most Costa Ricans are well-to-do when compared to the many destitute people found in neighboring countries.

Another thing setting Costa Ricans apart from other countries in the region is the cleanliness of its people. Costa Ricans take pride in their personal appearance. Men, women and children seem to be well dressed. Above all, you don't see as many ragged beggars and panhandlers as in Mexico and many other Latin American countries.

The people of Costa Rica also place great emphasis on education. More people can read and write in Costa Rica than in any other Central American country. A higher percentage of the population is enrolled in universities than in any other country in Latin America. Costa Ricans claim to have more school teachers than soldiers.

Costa Ricans are friendly and outgoing and will often go out of their way to help you even if you don't speak Spanish. They are also very pro-American and love anything American—music, TV, fashion and U.S. culture in general. Because of these close ties to the U.S. and just the right amount of American influence, Costa Ricans tend to be more like North Americans than any other people in Latin America.

Surprisingly they—especially the young people of the country— seem to have more liberal attitudes in some areas. Costa Rican women are considered to be some of the most sexually liberated females in Latin America. This liberal way of thinking can be due in part to the fact that the Catholic Church seems to have of a foothold in Costa Rican than in some other Latin American countries.

However, you should not get the wrong idea from reading this. The vast majority of the people are Catholic and can be conservative when it comes to such issues as movie censorship. Also, Costa Ricans don't miss the chance to celebrate the many religious holidays that occur throughout the year. (See Chapter 9 for a list of some of the most important holidays).

Generally speaking, the people of Costa Rica love to have fun, like to live with "gusto" and know how to enjoy themselves. One has only to go to any local dance hall on a weekend night to see *ticos* out having a good time, or observe entire families picnicing together on any given Sunday—the traditional family day in Costa Rica.

The people of Costa Rica, no matter what their station in life, seem to enjoy themselves with less and do not give as much importance to materialism as do North Americans. Even people who can't afford to, seem to be able to eat, drink, be merry and live for today.

Basic old-fashioned family values and unity are very important to Costa Ricans. Just as in the rest of Latin America a strong family unit seems to be the most important element in Costa Rican 's lives. Social life still centers around the home. Much of one's leisure time is usually spent with family. Mother's Day is one of the most important holidays. Parents and relatives go to almost any length to spoil and baby their children. Elderly family members are revered and generally treated better than their counterparts in the U.S. or Canada. Most are not sent to nursing homes as in the U.S. Young, adult, single children, especially women, tend to live with their families until they marry.

Costa Rican families will help each other through hard economic times and in the face of poverty. Some foreigners complain that it is difficult to develop deep friendships with Costa Ricans because the family unit is so strong and predominant.

Nepotism or using relatives and family conections to get ahead is the way things work in business and government in Costa Rica. In many instances it doesn't matter what your qualifications are, but who your family knows that helps you.

Despite all their admirable qualities, there is a negative side to the character of the Costa Rican people. While similar to North Americans in many ways and with a fondness for some aspects of *gringo* culture, Costa Ricans are distinctly Latin in their temperament. They suffer from many of the same problems endemic to all Latin American societies.

Corruption and bribery are a way of life; bureaucratic ineptitude and red-tape thrive; the concepts of punctuality and logical reasoning are almost non-existent by North American standards, and the "Mañana Syndrome"—of leaving for tomorrow what can be done today—seems to be the norm rather than the exception.

Unfortunately, as in most Latin American countries, **machismo** (manliness) is prevalent to some degree among Costa Rican males. *Machismo* is the belief in the natural superiority of men in all fields of endeavor. It becomes the obsession and constant preocupation of many Latin men to demonstrate they are *macho* in a variety of ways.

Fortunately, the Costa Rican version of *machismo* is much milder than the type found in Mexico, but it nevertheless exists.

There is no telling to what lengths some men will go in order to demonstrate their virility. A man's virility is measured by the number of seductions or *conquistas* he makes. It is not unusual for married men to have a *querida* or lover. Many even have children with their mistresses. Since many married men don't want to risk having a lover, they sleep with prostitutes or loose women called *zorras*.

For this reason many Costa Rican women prefer American men to Costa Rican men. As the Costa Rican women say, "Costa Rican men are *machista* and always have to prove it. You marry a Costa Rican man today and tomorrow he is out chasing other women and drinking!"

Costa Rica is said to have the highest rate of alcoholism in Central America — an estimated 20% of the population are problem drinkers. This should come as no surprise, since drinking is part of the *macho* mentality. Making love, drinking and flirting are the national pastimes of most Costa Rican men.

COSTA RICA'S LAND, HISTORY AND PEOPLE

As we discuss in Chapter 4, foreign women walking along the street will be alarmed by the flirtatious behavior and comments of some Costa Rican men. Many of these flirtations or *piropos*, as they are called in Spanish, may border on the obscene but are usually harmless forms of flattery to get a female's attention. Foreign women are wise to ignore this and any other manifestations of *machismo*.

Sadly, many Costa Ricans have misconceptions about North Americans' wealth. A few people seem to think that all Americans and Canadians are millionaires. It is easy to understand why many *ticos* think this way because of the heavy influence of the U.S. television and movies which depict North Americans as being very affluent. Also, the only contact many Costa Ricans have with Americans is primarily with tourists, who are usually living high on the hog and spending freely while on vacation.

It is therefore not surprising that some individuals will try to take advantage of foreigners by overcharging them for services and goods. Others will use very persuasive means to borrow amounts of money ranging from pocket change to larger sums of money, and have no intention of every paying the debt. Please, take our advice: don't lend money to anyone, however convincing their sob story.

Some foreigners, who have married Costa Rican women, have been "taken to the cleaners." Because family ties are so strong in Costa Rica , you can end up supporting your spouse's whole family.

We talked to one retired American who couldn't live on his two thousand dollar a month pension because he had to support not only his wife and stepchildren, but his wife's sister's children as well. Furthermore, he had to lend his father-in-law money to pay off a second mortgage because the bank was going to repossess the latter's house.

This is an extreme example, but we have heard many similar stories while living in Costa Rica. Not all Costa Rican families are like this one, but it doesn't hurt to be aware that the situation exists. Be careful with whom you get involved. (See Chapter 4 "Finding Companionship" for more on this subject).

When doing any business with Costa Ricans, you should excercise extreme caution. A few years ago we had the pleasure of dining with a prominent Costa Rican banker. We mentioned that we wanted start a business in Costa Rica. He replied, "Be very careful when doing business with Costa Ricans. This is not to say that all people are dishonest here. Just be cautious who you deal with."

We suggest that you don't dwell on these negatives and hope you realize how difficult it is to generalize about or stereotype any group of people.   After you have resided in Costa Rica and experienced living with the people, you will be able to make your own judgements.

The good qualities of the Costa Rican people far outweigh any shortcomings they may have. We have included this description of the Costa Rican people because any book about living in Costa Rica would be incomplete without it. To help you understand the Costa Rican people better, we suggest you read the book *The Costa Ricans* listed in the "Suggested Reading" section of this book.

CHAPTER TWO

The Economics of
Living in Costa Rica

HOW MUCH DOES IT COST TO LIVE IN COSTA RICA?

An important factor that determines the cost of living for foreigners in Costa Rica is their lifestyle. If you are used to a wealthy lifestyle, you spend more than someone accustomed to living frugally. But either way, you will still find Costa Rica to be a bargain.

Despite having one of the highest standards of living in Latin America, purchasing power is greater in Costa Rica than in the United States or Canada. We will explain the things that make this statement true.

San José's prices are the second lowest of any city's in the Americas, the cost of goods and services is among the lowest of any city's in the world. Housing costs only a fraction that it does in the U. S. and hired help is a steal. Utilities—telephone service, electricity, and water—are cheaper than in North America. You never need to heat your home or apartment because of Costa Rica's warm climate. You need not cook with gas, since most stoves are electric. These services cost about 30% of what they do at home. Bills for heating in the winter and air conditioning in the summer can cost hundreds of dollars in the states. Public transportation is also inexpensive. San José and surrounding suburbs occupy a very small area. A bus ride across town or to the suburbs usually costs from ten to twenty-five cents. Bus fares to the provinces costing no more than $10 to the farthest part in the country (see chapter 5). Taxi travel around San José is also inexpensive.

A gallon of regular gasoline costs about a dollar thirty-five, making Costa Rica's gasoline prices among the lowest in the Americas. Only oil-exporting countries like Mexico and Venezuela have cheaper gasoline. However, you don't really need a car because public transportation is so inexpensive. If you must have a new car for some reason, remember that new cars are very expensive due to high import duties. Because of this, people keep their cars for a long time and take good care of them. We recommend buying used cars since they are usually in good mechanical condition and their resale value is excellent. Food, continuing education, entertainment (movies cost about two dollars) and, above all, health care, are surprisingly affordable. You'll find more about these benefits later on.

When you have lived in Costa Rica a while, learned the ins-and-outs and made some friends and contacts, you can cut your living costs more by sharing a house or apartment, house-sitting in exchange for free rent, investing in high-interest yielding accounts in one of Costa Rica's many banks, working full or part-time (if you can find legal work), starting a small business or bartering within the expatriate community, doing without packaged and canned imported brand-name foods, eating in small cafes or *sodas* instead of expensive restaurants, or buying fresh foods in bulk at the Central Market like Costa Ricans do. You can also help yourself by learning how to get a better rate of exchange on your money, and by learning Spanish so you can bargain and get lower prices when shopping.

Taking all of the aforementioned and personal life-styles into consideration, the minimum needed for a decent standard of living for a single person ranges from $600 to $1000 monthly. You can indeed live for as little as $30 a day. Some single people scrape by on considerably less and others spend hundreds of dollars more, again depending on what one is accustomed to. A couple can live well on $1200 per month, and live in luxury for $2000. Couples with husband and wife both receiving good pensions can live even better. Remember, two in Costa Rica, can often live as cheaply as one. Any way you look at it, you will enjoy a higher standard of living in Costa Rica and get more for your money. Consider that the average Costa Rican earns only $150--$250 a month.

When you take into account all these factors and such intangibles as: good year-round weather, the friendly Costa Rican people, the lack of political strife and serious violent crime (no society is crime free), and a more peaceful way of life—no price is too high to pay for living in a unique, tropical paradise like Costa Rica.

THE ECONOMICS OF LIVING IN COSTA RICA

Before closing this section, we want to emphasize that you should not be alarmed by high real estate prices you may hear about or see advertised in the *Tico Times* or *Costa Rica Today*. This recent rise in land prices results from the current land boom and increasing popularity of Costa Rica. Inflated real estate prices do not reflect the real cost of living in Costa Rica, which is still relatively low when compared to the Canada, Europe and the U.S. Even more important, the Costa Rican government must keep the cost of goods and services affordable for the Costa Rican people in order to avoid the social problems found in most other Latin American Countries.

Approximate Cost of Living and Prices as of March 1995 in Dollars*

Rentals - Monthly

House (small, unfurnished) $200
House (large, luxurious) $1000–1200
Apartment (small, 1–2 bedrooms, unfurnished .... $125+
Apartment (large, luxurious) .... $400+
Property Taxes .... $30 a year on a small home

Home Prices

House (small) .... $30,000+
House (large) .... $80,000+

Miscellaneous   Monthly

Electric Bill (apt.) $15–25
Water-Sewage (apt.) $8
Telephone (calls within the country) $10
Cable TV $30

Taxi .... ¢100 first kilometer, and ¢45 thereafter per kilometer
Bus Fares (around city) .... $.25
Gasoline (regular gas) .... $1.36 per gallon
Gasoline (super) .... $1.50 per gallon
Gasoline (diesel) .... $1.13 per gallon
Maid/Gardener .... $1.25 per hour
Restaurant Meal (inexpensive) .... $5.00+

Soda (a diner or coffee shop) Meal $2.00
Restaurant (mid-range) $10.00

Banana .... $.5
Soft drink .... $.38
Pineapple $1.00
Papaya .... $.70
Lettuce .... $.20
Orange .... $.8
Rice (1lb.) .... $.45
Steak .... $4.60 lb.
Quart of Milk .... $.95
Beer .... $.50 to $.75
Airmail Letter .... around $.30 to the U.S.

Doctor's Visit $15–35
Nation Health Insurance ...... $450.00 yearly for permanent residents
New Automobile .... $20,000–$50,000

* These prices are subject to fluctuations.

• Corporate Resource Consulting firm that compares costs of goods and services, rates San José among the least expensive cost-of -living cities in the world and second to Quito, Ecuador in the Americas.

INVESTING IN COSTA RICA

A recent study by the *Miami Herald* rated Costa Rica the 27th safest counry for investment of 140 countries surveyed. If you are not impressed by Costa Rica's ranking, consider that the U.S. was ranked only 22nd!

Let's review a few of the reasons Costa Rica has such magnetism for qualified foreign investors. First, and perhaps most important is the enduring political stability. As you already know Costa Rica has had a strong, democratic government without interruption since the

1940s and an excellent centralized banking system. The trend towards an open economy and possible trade pacts with such nations as the U.S. and Mexico are conducive to investment in Costa Rica. There are also no government expropriations or interference as in many Latin American countries.

Costa Rica is easily accessible from all parts of the world by land, sea or air. Outstanding phone, telex and telegraph systems link Costa Rica internationally to other communication networks. Also, let's remember that investors in Costa Rica have equal rights and laws to protect them. Furthermore, many opportunities await foreigners who start new businesses previously nonexistant in Costa Rica. Finally, as you will see, the cost of labor is low.

Many attractive incentives are available to foreigners investing in Costa Rica. Investments of $50,000 or more in an approved project qualify the investor for legal residency. However, it is not necessary to become a resident to own or manage a business. Anyone who owns a business can import many items used to operate it and get a tax break on some of the usual duties. Contact the incentive section of the **Costa Rican Tourist Institute (I.C.T.)** for more information about incentive programs.

Tourism is now the leading industry in Costa Rica. Many opportunities exist in this field but even more bureaucracy and competition. Small hotels and bread-and-breakfasts were good investments a few years ago, but there may be a surplus of them now. We have a good friend who refurbished an old building and turned it into a small hotel in 1990. He has done very well only because he has been in the country for a while, knows all the ropes and was a pioneer in the field.

Foreigners can invest with Costa Rica's nationalized banking system, private banks or finance companies. Interest rates are higher than in the United States (22 percent or even higher) and there are many attractive savings accounts and time deposit programs to choose from. There are some degrees of bank secrecy, liberal money transfer regulations and favorable tax laws for foreigners (see the section in this chapter titled "Taxes").

Foreigners can also invest in the local Stock Exchange (**Bolsa Nacional de Valores**) to get better returns than from tradition financial systems.

Costa Rica has the largest stock exchange in Central America. Around twenty firms are registered with the National Stock Exchange. Costa Rican stock brokers can study economic trends and give you advice on investing in government bonds, real estate, time deposits and other investments.

The Costa Rican Stock Exchange is regulated by the National Securities Comission, which is the counterpart of the U.S. Securities and Exchange Comission. They can give you information about the reliability of firms and brokers.

If you are seriously interested in investing in Costa Rica, we suggest that you get a copy of *The Investors Guide to Costa Rica,* which is available through the **Costa Rican-American Chamber of Commerce or AMCHAM.** A monthly magazine titled, *Business in Costa Rica* also has advice on how to invest in Costa Rica. You may want to attend a meeting of the Investors Club of Costa Rica. For information call 240-2240 or 222 -5601.

The PropData company specializes in helping foreigners interested in investing in Costa Rica. They have a professional team of experienced English-speaking business consultants, a real estate data base and provide numerous technical and financial services. Their address and phone number are listed below.

Before investing you should take the time to do your homework. Under no circumstances should you invest right off the plane, that is to say, on your first trip to Costa Rica. Unscrupulous individuals will always prey on impulsive buyers anywhere in the world. Be wary of any sales men who try to pressure you into investing. We also suggest you ask a lot of questions and get information and and assistance from any of these organizations:

American Chamber of Commerce of Costa Rica: AMCHAM
P.O. Box 4946

San José, Costa Rica

Tel: 011-506-233-1133; Fax: 001-506-223-2349

                or

Miami mailing address:

SJO 1576

P.O. Box 025216

Miami, FL. 33102-5216

Coalition for Investment Initiatives-CINDE
P.O. Box 7170

San José, Costa Rica

Tel: 011-506-220-0036; Fax: 011-506-220-4750

Export Promotion Center - CENPRO
P.O. Box 5418
San José, Costa Rica
Tel: 001-506-220-0066; Fax: 011-506-223-5722
The Costa Rican Stock Exchange
Bolsa Nacional de Valores
P.O. Box 1756
San José, Costa Rica
Tel: 011-506-222-8011; Fax: 011-506-255-0531
National Securities Commission
P.O. Box 10058
San José, Costa Rica
Tel: 011-506-233-2840; Fax: 011-506-233-0969
Canada Costa Rica Chamber of Commerce
Tel: 011-506-257-3241
PropData
SJO Dept. 2052
P.O. Box 025216
Miami, Florida USA 33102-5216
Tel: 011-506-233-6435; Fax: 011-506-255-4611

TIPPING

A 15 percent sales tax, as well as a three percent tourist tax ia added to all hotelbills.. Cafes and restaurants include a 10 percent tip, so tipping above that amount is not necessary. Of course, employees such as bellhops and taxi drivers are appreciative of any additional gratuity for excellent service.

INEXPENSIVE HOUSING

Housing is affordable and plentiful in Costa Rica. With the exception of downtown San José, rents for houses or apartments are reasonable— half or less the cost in the United States. Depending on location and personal taste, a small house or large apartment usually rents for a few hundred dollars per month.

A luxurious house or apartment will go for $600 to $1000 per month or even higher. Most Costa Ricans pay less than $150 monthly for rent, a few hundred dollars should rent a nice place to live.

Most houses and apartments have all the amenities of home: large bedrooms, bathrooms with hot water, kitchens, dining rooms, a laundry room and even maid's quarters, since help is so inexpensive in Costa Rica.

If you can't afford to buy a house in the U.S. or Canada, prices of homes begin at around $30,000 with limited financing available. However, it's a good idea to pay cash or find your financing from abroad, since interest rates are very high.

You don't have to be a resident of Costa Rica to own property there and you're entitled to the same ownership rights as citizens of Costa Rica.

Unlike Mexico some beach front property may be purchased. But you can no longer buy or build within 200 meters of the high tide line unless there is existing housing or a new tourisim project involved. This 200 meter zone is called The Maritime Zone or *Zona Marítima*.

For your information, beach front property is being bought-up fast, and the price of this and other prime real estate is soaring—with much of it being overpriced.

Before you move to the beach, you should know that the novelty of living at the beach wears off fast. Visiting the beach for a few days or weeks is very different from living there full-time. The humidity, boredom, lack of emergency medical facilities and the general incoveniences of living in an often out-of-the-way area, are factors to consider before moving to any beach area.

Besides homes and beach propery there are also condominiums, farms, lots and ranches for sale at reasonable prices, depending on their location.

You will be pleased to know that no capital gains taxes on real estate exist in Costa Rica, so it is an excellent investment. You do have to pay yearly taxes, but they are low by U.S. standards. Yearly property taxes are on a sliding scale up to 1.17% of the stated value of a particular property. The tax is based on a figure far below the market value or sales price of a property.

If you decide to buy real estate an attorney is absolutely necessary to do the legal work for purchasing property. We strongly recommend that your lawyer do a thorough search of all records before you make your purchase and make sure there are no encumbrances (*gravámenes*) on it. You can obtain information about property at the ***Registro de***

THE ECONOMICS OF LIVING IN COSTA RICA

Propiedades (like our recorder's office) in the suburb of Zapote, about five minutes from downtown San José by car or taxi. You can also find the status and ownership of a piece of property and get any title documents and surveys you may need at this office.

Before you buy property, your lawyer should explain the legalities of buying and selling property in Costa Rica. **Be sure you do not hire the same lawyer used by the seller of land.** Also, don't forget to check that you are buying the land from its rightful owner. Some owners have sold their land to several buyers. You can protect your real estate investment further if you talk with neighbors about water shortages, safety and burglaries in the area.

Remember, always see the property in person and never buy sight unseen. Don't forget to make sure there are no problems with squatters and check to see if you need special permits to build. Be sure to check the comparative land values in your area to see if you are getting a good deal, and that roads, electricity and telephone service are available if you are thinking of living in a remote area. If you can't live on your property year-round, then you will have to hire a guard or a reliable housesitter to watch it for you.

Also, we suggest that you rent for at least six months. Make sure to buy where it's easy to rent or sell your home or condominium, in case you change your plans or in the event of a personal emergency.

To find an apartment, house or land to purchase look for listings in the *Tico Times* and *Costa Rica Today* or inquire at one of the real estate or rental agencies in downtown San José. Better yet, talk to other retirees.

If you want to save money, look in the local Spanish newspapers *La Nación* or *La República* because prices are usually lower. Also, keep in mind that housing costs are much higher in *gringo* enclaves like Escazú and Rohrmoser. Be sure to keep in mind that the farther away you live from San José and other cities the more you get for your money.

In Costa Rica you can build your retirement dream house, if you so desire, since land, labor and materials are inexpensive. However, think twice about undertaking such a project, because you could be flirting with disaster.

Many retirees, who have built homes complain that it sounds easier than it really is. They would not do it again because of costly delays, unreliable labor, fussy building inspectors, different laws and building codes and many other unforeseen problems. Be sure to talk with foreigners who have built homes to see what obstacles they encountered.

You may want to use the services of a real estate broker to buy or sell property in Costa Rica. In order to find a competent, honest broker, it is wise to talk to other expatriates or contact the local Chamber of Real Estate Brokers or *Cámara Costarricense de Bienes Raíces*. But be careful because the real estate industry is not regulated as in the U.S. In the back of this book we list several real estate agencies in the San José area.

If you are interested in purchasing real estate for investment purposes, you will be pleased to know that the government welcomes your investment.

Whether you are buying a home or an investment property, you are bound to make money, if you hang on to your property. Real estate values are expected to double over the next decade or two. There is limited land in some urban areas, so the resale value goes up as population grows. Beach property will be a good investment because of the demand.

Before buying a home or making any other real estate investment, we suggest you educate yourself by studying the Costa Rican real estate market. Fortunately, there are three new books available to assist you and answer most of your questions.

Purchasing Real Estate in Costa Rica, by Alvaro Carballo, a noted Costa Rican attorney and real estate specialist, is intended to reduce the anxiety of buying real estate in a foreign country. It is very informative and complete.

Bill Baker's, *The Rules of the Game: Buying Real Estate In Costa Rica,* is another gem. Anyone considering purchasing real estate in Costa Rica will find this book extremely valuable. It is full of useful information and contains samples of standard real estate forms used to make most transactions. You shouldn't consider making any real estate investment without reading this great book.

If you are interested in income producing property, you should read Frank Thomas Gallardo's, *Developing and Managing Profitable Rental Real Estate in Costa Rica.* It covers almost everything you need to know about the subject. The author has many years of experience investing in Costa Rican real estate.

* If you are interested in obtaining any of these books, see the appendix of this book for details.

AFFORDABLE HIRED HELP

As you know full or part-time domestic help, is hard to find and prohibitively expensive for the average person, not to mention a retire, in the United States. This is not the case in Costa Rica. A live-in maid or other full-time help usually costs between $150 and $200 per month. Often you can hire a couple for a bargain price with the woman working as a maid and the man working as a full-time gardener and watchman.

In Costa Rica a maid usually does everything from washing clothes to taking care of small children. You can also use your maid to stand in line for you or run errands and bargain for you in stores, since foreigners often pay more for some items because of their naivety and poor language skills.

General handymen and carpenters are also inexpensive. If you are infirm, one of the above people can assist you with many daily tasks. To find quality help, check with other retirees for references or look in local newspapers. (*The Tico Times*, La *República* or La *Nación*).

Costa Rica's labor laws for domestic workers are strict and difficult to interpret. All domestic employees have the right to social security benefits from the *Caja Costarricense de Seguro Social* (roughly the equivalent of our Social Security System). This important institution pays for sick leave, general health care, disability pensions and maternity care.

It is the employer's responsibility to pay monthly social security payments for each employee. The employer must make monthly payments of about 20 percent of the worker's monthly wage. In return the worker is entitled to social security services mentioned above.

New employees must be registered with social security within a week of being hired. All new employees must register in an office in downtown San José (Tel: 223-9890).

Employers must also pay minimum wage to employees. This wage is set by the Ministry of Labor (Tel: 223-7166) and depends on the job and skills required. Wages average about $100 per month. Live-in help can receive an additional 50 percent more that is not actually paid to them but is used when computing certain benefits and bonuses.

Live-in domestic help cannot be required to work more than twelve hours a day, although few expect this. Live-in workers usually work- eight hours a day like other workers. Most regular employees work an eight hour day, five days per week. Live-in employees can work more than this but have to be given some time off.

Furthermore, employees are entitled to a paid vacation depending on their length of employment and whether they are full or part-time.

Employers must also pay *aguinaldo* or Christmas bonus if an employee has worked from December 1 through November 30. It is the equivalent of one month's salary. This Christmas bonus should be paid in early December. Don't forget that live-in employees receive an additional 50 percent Christmas bonus.

A maternity leave one month before a baby's birth is required; the employee receives 50percent of her normal salary.

In some cases it is the employer's responsibility to pay severance pay, all accumulated, unused vacation time, the proportionate *aguinaldo* and any wages due when a worker is terminated.

An employee must be given notice prior to being laid off. Severance pay is usually one month's salary for each year worked. If an employee resigns voluntarily, the employer doesn't owe severance pay. For your information, severance pay is called *prestaciones*.

We have touched only briefly on the main points of Costa Rican labor law, because it is very complex. If you have any questions, we advise you to contact the Minister of Labor (223-7166) or better yet your attorney. Have your lawyer help with any labor related matters to avoid unnecessary problems arising between you and your hired help.

To give you an idea of what salaries are like in Costa Rica, here are some samples of the approximate starting mininum monthly wages as established by the Labor Ministry or *Ministerio de Trabajo y Seguridad Social* (Tel: 221-7166): Accountant $400.00, bus driver $200.00, chauffer $175.00, clerk $175.00, computer operator $300.00, dentist or doctor $1000.00, other professionals $430.00, farm hand $125.00, domestic worker $120.00, executive bilingual secretary $375.00, guard $180.00, journalist $550.00, messenger $$175.00, nurse $375.00, plant supervisor $400.00, phone operator $170.00, secretary $200.00, and unskilled laborer $150.00.

Only inexperienced workers receive these starting salaries. Experienced workers command higher wages. However, keep in mind that these figures vary and are subject to change at any time. Such factors as bonuses and other perks also increase actual salaries.

MEDICAL CARE

Costa Ricans are proud of their nation's achievements in the field of health care. Their up-to-date, affordable state-run system reaches all levels of society by offering the same medical treatment to the poor as those with greater resources. Hospitals, clinics and complete medical services are available in all major cities and some towns.

Many international medical athorities rate Costa Rica as having one of the best, low-cost medical care systems in the world when preventive and curative medicine are considered.

The infant mortality rate in Costa Rica is lower than that in the United States, and life expectancy is as high as if not higher. Hospitals have the latest equipment and laboratories are excellent. You can feel safe having most operations without returning to the U.S. or Canada. Most surgical proceedures cost only a fraction of what they do in the U.S.

Public medical facilities are so good that you don't usually need private care. Most private specialists are required by law to work part-time in public hospitals. However, private clinics and hospitals do provide quicker services with more privacy enabling you to avoid long lines and the bureaucracy of the public system.

The **Clinica Bíblica** (Tel: 223-6422), in downtown San José, is a first-class private hospital with an excellent coronary unit. The **Clínica Católica** (Tel: 225-5055), in Guadalupe, a suburb of San José, is another fine private hospital with complete hospital and emergency services. The **Clínica Santa Rita** (Tel: 221-6433), near the court buildings, has a an excellent maternity center. The **Hospital Cristano Jerusalem** (Tel: 285-0202), in the Alto de Guadalupe, offers limited services. Although not a hospital, the **Clínica Americana** (Tel: 222-1010), next to the Clínica Bíblica, offers private out-patient service and U.S.- trained doctors, who are on call 24-hours a day.

If you have to enter a private hospital, costs will generally be well under a hundred dollars a day. This includes a spacious private room and bathroom, usually a T.V. and an extra bed or sofa-bed so a relative may spend the night, if necessary.

We know an American who spent a couple of days in the private Clínica Católica hospital and said, "The attention was first class, the food was as good as home cooking and the same care would have cost thousands of dollars in the states." It is important to know that payment can be made at most hospitals and clinics with any major credit card. Foreign medical insurance is not accepted, but you can get a reimbursement from your health insurance company, if they cover you abroad.

Most Costa Rican doctors are excellent and have been trained in Europe, Canada or the United States. If you don't speak Spanish, you don't have to worry since many local doctors speak English, but most receptionists and nurses do not.

Doctor's fees for office visits vary. A good private specialist usually charges between $15 and $30 for each visit, although some doctors charge a little more and others a little less. If you join Costa Rica's national health care system, you don't have to pay for each office visit, only a small monthly membership fee. If you have any questions about medical fees or doctors you can consult the *Colegio de Médicos*, which is the Costa Rican equivalent of the AMA. To find a good English speaking physician or specialist talk to other retirees, look in the Yellow Pages under *Médicos* or look for doctor's ads in the *Tico Times*.

The quality of dental work in Costa Rica is equal to that in Europe, Canada or the U.S. On the average, dental work costs about 25 percent to 30 percent less than in the U.S. Most dentists charge around $35 for an initial exam. Here are the approximate costs of the most common cosmetic procedures: wisdom tooth surgery $175; single root canal $120; new crown $250; and tooth extraction $30. Check prices with the dentist of your choice, since rates vary.

Cosmetic surgery is inexpensive in Costa Rica and Costa Rica's surgeons are among the world's best. People from all over the world flock to Costa Rica for cosmetic surgery because prices are lower than in the U.S. for comparable procedures. Furthermore, Costa Rica's plastic surgeons are trained in the U.S. or Europe. They keep up-to-date on new trends and methods in their field and attend professional seminars regularly. Rates for different operations vary from doctor to doctor. You can combine several procedures to reduce the price substantially. There are even package prices that combine surgery, hotel and hospitalization.

The cost of a face lift is between $2000-$3,500; nose surgery around $2000; liposuction $800-$1,500; and eyelid surgery between $800-$1,500. Again, rates will vary from surgeon to surgeon.

We suggest you contact any of the doctors we have listed in this book. They will be more than happy to send a brochure and answer any of your questions.

THE ECONOMICS OF LIVING IN COSTA RICA

Costa Rica's health care system is available to retirees (*pensionados*) and other foreign residents. They may join the **Caja Costarricense de Seguro Social** (Costa Rican Social Security System) and enjoy the same free medical attention as most Costa Ricans do. Depending on age and sex, the annual cost for Seguro Social ranges between $200 and $400 for a single person. There is a discount if more than one person is insured on the same policy. It is easy to enroll an entire family for a low monthly rate. So, retirees and other residents need not worry about lacking adequate medical coverge in Costa Rica.

A new type of medical insurance is now offered through the Residents Association, to supplement the government's Social Security system. This plan is excellent. For a few hundred dollars a year a man or woman between 50 and 70 can get a yearly coverage of almost $35,000. This program, in conjunction with the government Social Security system, should provide more than ample medical coverage especially when you consider the low cost of health care in Costa Rica.

While checking out Costa Rica as a tourist, to see if it is the place for you to settle, you can get temporary medical insurance through the Costa Rican Social Security office and the **International Organization of Cultural Interchanges (O.I.C.I.)** This insurance may be bought at many travel agencies, language schools or tourism offices. If you plan to reside in the country for more than one month and have your tourist visa and other papers are up to date, contact the O.I.C.I. office on the fourth floor of the Mendiola building on Avenida Central, or call 222-7867.

If you want to get complete information on the Costa Rican medical system, read the book, *Medical Systems of Costa Rica*. The author , the late Frank Chalfont, a long-time resident of the country was familiar with Costa Rica's public and private medical systems. See the appendix for information on ordering this book.

Pharmacies are numerous in Costa Rica and they stock most standard medicines available in Europe, Canada and the U.S. Some pharmacies remain open 24-hours a day are in downtown San José at **Clínica Bíblica Hospital**, 223-6422; at the **Clínica Católica Hospital,** 225-9095; and at the **Clínica Santa Rita**, 221-64-33. The **Fischel** pharmacy 223-0909, across from the main post office in San José, is open 24-hours a day. It sometimes has a doctor on duty to give medical advice. Fichel's will deliver medicine and prescriptions in the San José area.

Many medicines available only by prescription in the U.S. can be purchased over-the-counter at any local *farmacia.* In Costa Rica pharmacists are permitted to prescribe medicines as well as administer on-the-spot injections. In general, most medicines are 50 percent their cost in the United States.

In Costa Rica there is also full service custodial health care available for the elderly (men and women alike) at a very low cost. Care for less independent senior citizens is around $1000 per month. Retirements Centers International offers comprehensive medical care and assistance which includes all medicines, lab work, dental care, physical therapy, rehabilitation and special diets.

These programs are some of Central America's best and are considerably less expensive than in the United States. However, if these facilities are beyond an elderly person's means, a full-time live-in domestic worker can be hired as a nurse for a couple of hundred dollars monthly. In addition to caring for an infirm person this worker can manage other household chores.

For additional information contact:

RETIREMENT CENTERS INTERNATIONAL
Apdo. 2627-1000 San José, Costa Rica, Central America
Telephone 506-222-10-55

HOGAR RETIRO PARA ANCIANOS SAN PEDRO
Apdo. 52250, Tres Rios, Costa Rica

HOTELES GERIATRICOS
Apdo. 2140-1000, San José, Costa Rica

HOGAR DE ANCIANOS PEDRO CLAVER
Apdo. 441, San José, Costa Rica

GOLDEN VALLEY HACIENDA
Tel: 506-443-8575

VILLA CONFORT GERIATRIC
Tel: 506-443-8191

EMILY'S CHATEAU CONVALESCENT HOME
Apartado 1261-3000, Heredia, Costa Rica
Tel: 506-268-8780

In the U.S. contact:

P.O. Box 1592
South Gate, CA 90280-1592
Tel: (213) 773-7176

THE'ECONOMICS OF LIVING IN COSTA RICA

* Once again, to find a good physician or specialist talk to other retirees, look in the yellow pages under *MEDICOS* or look for doctors' ads in the *Tico Times* and *Costa Rica Today.* Below are the names of some English speaking physicians and dentists.

Dr. Arturo Acosta—Dentist
P.O. Box 906-1250, Escazú, Costa Rica
Tel: 506-228-9904; Fax: 506-444-500

Dr. John Anastasi P.—Chiropractor. Tel: 506- 231-3165

Miguel Alfaro Davila—Cosmetic Surgery
P.O. Box 1813 San José, Costa Rica
Tel: 506-222-1454

Dr. Willy Feinzaig—Urology
P.O. Box 110-1000, San José, Costa Rica
Tel: 506- 222-1010; Fax: 506- 231-2867

Dr. Arnoldo Fournier—Plastic Surgery
P.O. Box 117-1002, San José, Costa Rica
Tel: 506- 222-5160; Fax: 506- 255-4370

Dr. Ronald Pass Jimenez—Family Dentistry
P.O. Box 2463-1000, San José, Costa Rica
Tel: 506- 228-9933; Fax: 506- 228-9931

Dr. Alejandro Lev—Plastic Surgery
P.O. Box 183-1007, San José, Costa Rica
Tel: 506-221-8329

Dr. Joaquín Martínez—Ophthalmology
Tel: 506-289-7418; Fax: 506-238-0005

Dr. Rudolf Nuñez—Clinical Dermatology
Tel: 506-222-6265; Fax: 506-257-0244

Dr. Ronald Pino—Cosmetic Surgery
P.O. Box 447-1007 San José, Costa Rica
Tel: 506-220-0224; Fax: 506-231-6017

Dr. Manuel Trimiño Vásquez—Physician/Psychiatrist
He has many clients from the U.S. and is bilingual.
Tel: 506-221-6140 or 506-233-3333

For the names of more doctors and dentists, see the section in the back of this book titled " More Phone Numbers."

FINDING WORK IN COSTA RICA

We have some discouraging news for those living on small pensions and hoping to supplement their income with a part-or full-time job or for others who need to work just to keep busy. Finding work can be difficult, but not impossible. In the first place, it is not easy for a Costa Rican, not to mention foreigners who don't speak fluent Spanish, to find permanent work.

If you are one of the few foreigners who has mastered Spanish, you will probably have a fair chance of finding work in tourism or some other related field. However, your best bet may be to find employment with a North American firm doing business in Costa Rica. You may be able to find a job as a salesman or a representative.

Even if you know little or no Spanish, you have a chance of finding work as an English teacher at a language institute in San José. Don't expect to earn more than a survival salary from one of these jobs because the minimum wage in Costa Rica is low. Working as a full-time language instructor won't bring you more than a few hundred dollars monthly. As supplemental income or busywork, this is fine, but you won't make a living given the kind of life style you are probably accustomed to.

Try putting one of your skills to use by providing some service to the large expatriate community in Costa Rica. For example, if you are a writer or journalist you might look for work at one of Costa Rica's two English language newspapers. Unfortunately, if you are a retired professional such as a doctor or lawyer, you can't practice in Costa Rica because of certain restrictions but can offer your services as a consultant to other foreigners and retirees.

As if finding work were not hard enough in Costa Rica, a work permit or residency is required before foreigners can work legally. Labor laws are very strict and the government doesn't want foreigners taking jobs away from Costa Ricans. You are only allowed to work if you can perform specialized work that a Costa Rican can't.

However, many foreigners work for under-the-table pay without a work permit. This practice is illegal, but you can do so at your own risk if you want to bear the consequences. If you don't seek remuneration, you can always find volunteer work to keep yourself busy. This kind of work is legal, so you don't need a work permit or run the risk of being deported for working illegally.

STARTING A BUSINESS

As a foreigner, you can invest in Costa Rica and even start your own business with only some restrictions.

As we stated earlier in this chapter, Costa Rica is ripe for innovative foreigners willing to take a risk and start businesses that have not previously existed. However, running a business in Costa Rica is not like managing a business in the United States because of unusual labor laws, the Costa Rican work ethic and the Costa Rican way of doing business.

In order for a foreigner to own a businesses, a Costa Rican corporation or *Sociedad Anónima* must be formed (see the section titled "Taxes" in this chapter).

If you do choose to establish your own business, keep in mind that you can be limited to managerial or supervisory duties and will have to hire Costa Ricans to do the bulk of everyday work. We also recommend that you do a thorough feasibility study. Don't assume that what works in the U.S. will work in Costa Rica. Check out restrictions and the tax situation. And most important, choose a business in which you have a vast prior experience.

During the time we have lived in Costa Rica, we have seen many foreigners succeed and fail in business ventures. About three in ten foreigners succeed in business in Costa Rica. There are some benefits to investing in certain businesses in Costa Rica. As we mention in Chapter 8, you can obtain Costa Rican Residency by investing in tourism or a reforestation project. Also, part of your profits can be sheltered in your corporation.

After reading the above, if you still have questions or are confused, we advise you to consult a knowledgeable Costa Rican attorney for further information.

MONEY

The *colón*, named for Christopher Columbus, is Costa Rica's official currency. One of the most stable currencies in Latin America, the *colón* has recently been somewhat shaky because of devaluations. Fortunately, the devaluations are relatively small when compared to the mega-devaluations and run-away inflation rampant in other Latin American countries. Since your main source of income will probably be in dollars, you should not worry too much about devaluations unless you have large amounts of money in *colones*, which is not advisable for long-term investments. Devaluations can be good because they increase your purchasing power until prices catch up. The rate of exchange, which is set by the Central Bank, was around 165 colones per dollar as of January 1995.

BLUE BILLS	¢5000
RED BILLS	¢1000
ORANGE BILLS	¢500
GRAY BILLS	¢100
LIGHT GREEN BILLS	¢50

A new ¢50 *colón* coin, has been issued to replace Costa Rica's lowest denomination bill.

You can exchange money at most banks between 9 a.m. and 4 p.m. Monday through Friday. When you exchange money at a bank, do so early in the morning because lines can be long later in the day and you can wait for what seems to be an eternity. You should always carry your passport or *pensionado* I.D. when exchanging money or for other banking transactions. When banks are closed, you can change money at a special office in downtown San José under the Plaza de la Cultura, open Saturday 9 a.m. to 3 p.m. and on Sundays, 9 a.m. to 1 p.m., and on some holidays. Also, most hotels can change traveler's checks or dollars.

Money can also be changed on the black market where you get a better rate of exchange than in the banks. Black market money changers operate along Avenida Central between Calles 2 and 4, in the vicinity of the Post Office. You don't have to look for these money changers since they usually approach you. Many people prefer to change their money this way because all transactions are quick and there are no lines as in the banks. Once you have been in Costa Rica for a while some of these money changers will get to know you and may do the majority of your transactions.

Be careful of slick change artists who may be distributing counterfeit bills or attempt to shortchange you.

Some money changers work discretely from their own offices in the same area of town. We recommend the **Villalobos Brothers Money Traders**, who have a large clientele of retirees and other foreigners. In addition to changing money, they cash personal and social security checks and provide many other related services. Their office is located 75 meters south of the main Post Office next to the Banco Lyon, on the second floor of the Schyfter Building. Tel: 506-233-0090 or 233-3127; Fax: 223-8838.

BANKING

There are branches of Costa Rica's state-owned banks in San José and other large cities and towns. The headquarters of Costa Rica's largest banks **El Banco Nacional, El Banco de Costa Rica** and **El Banco Central** are in downtown San José near the Central Post Office.

It is advisable to open an account at one of these banks, so you can have a dollar account to protect against unexpected currency devaluations, cash personal checks, obtain a safety deposit box for some of your valuables and facilitate having money sent to you from abroad. Regarding the latter, you should make sure that the bank you choose works with a U.S. correspondent bank to avoid untimely delays in cashing checks.

Other banking services are 24-hour automated tellers that disperse a few hundred dollars at a time from your account, high-yield certificates of deposit in *colones*, and credit card services. By the way, most banks are normally open from 9 a.m. to 3 p.m.

Warning: Never plan to do any banking on the second or last Friday of the month since it's pay day for most Costa Rican workers and lines sometimes extend outside the bank.

TAXES

You will have many tax advantages in Costa Rica. Investors pay no capital gains taxes on real estate investments there. High interest-bearing bank accounts are also tax free. The maximum Costa Rican tax rate is around 30 percent with no city or state taxes and low property taxes. Furthermore, you can form a Costa Rican "offshore" corporation, or *Sociedad Anónima*, to shelter your earnings.

Briefly a *Sociedad Anónima* is an anonymous corporation anyone, even tourists, can set up without their name's appearing on any records. The initials S.A. will appear after a corporation's name instead of Inc. A Costa Rican corporation is similar to its U.S. counterpart in having a board of directors, share holders and shares which can be bought and sold freely. You control all the stock in the corporation but your identity remains unknown. You're able to maintain some degree of secrecy in financial matters and protect youself from some taxes problems.

These offshore corporations are used in most business transactions within Costa Rica and abroad. Because they are foreigr corporations they are not subject to U.S. taxes. Furthermore, Costa Rican corporations pay only minimal taxes in Costa Rica or none at all.

Contact your attorney if you are seriously thinking about forming one of these anonymous corporations. Your lawyer can explain how these corporations work and why they have advantages and disadvantages. The fee for starting one of these corporations is usually between $300 and $1000.

You will have to pay taxes on income earned in Costa Rica. *La Tributación Directa*, the local eqivalent of the IRS, is in charge of collecting taxes, but is far less efficient. However, if you go into business in Costa Rica and form a tax sheltered corporation, most of your expenses can be written off.

Also, unlike some other places, a foreign retiree is not required to pay Costa Rican taxes on his external income (income generated abroad), so you can see why Costa Rica is considered a tax-haven by many people.

You must file your U.S. income tax returns yearly through the American Embassy. You have to declare all income earned abroad, but you may claim a tax exemption up to $ 70,000 on overseas-earned income. Fortunately, if you reside outside the U.S. you may wait to file your taxes until June 15th.

If you have any tax questions, contact the U.S. Embassy or IRS. Call either the Consular Section of the U.S. Embassy, 220-3939 or the nearest IRS office in Mexico City at 525 211-0042, ext. 3557.

If you need help with your tax forms and returns while living in Costa Rica, contact the local H&R Block, 231-1004. You can also call Gordon Finwall, a tax attorney and C.P.A. living in Costa Rica at 224-1351, David Houseman at 223-2787 or 239-2045 and Robert McBeath at 233-0348 for income tax assistance or for help with IRS problems.

Canadians will have to contact the local Canadian Consulate at 011-506-255-3522 to their tax obligations while living abroad.

INSURANCE

In Costa Rica all insurance is less expensive than in the United States. Auto, fire and theft insurance will cost less than half the U.S. premium. If you own an automobile, Costa Rican insurance is compulsory and must be paid for when you register your car. This mandatory liability insurance, *seguro obligatorio*, has to be renewed yearly, then you recieve a decal or *marchamo* for your car.

For an additional cost supplemental insurance policies provide broader coverage than basic compulsory policy. Your car's value determines the price of your premium.

We have already mentioned the affordability of medical insurance in Costa Rica in the section titled "Medical Care."

The Instituto Nacional de Seguros or INS, as it is called, handles all of your insurance needs. However, because not everyone's insurance needs are the same and because laws and coverages work differently in Costa Rica, we suggest you consult your attorney or the English speaking insurance agent, Dave Garrett, we have listed below. He just finished a booklet titled, *Insurance in Costa Rica*.

It is an excellent introduction to the Costa Rican insurance system for foreigners who have recently moved to Costa Rica or those thinking of doing so. This handy book goes into detail on most kinds of insurance, including car, fire, theft, life, medical.

Commercial insurance is not included. It also has a handy glossary of Spanish insurance terms and is full of practical tips.

To purchase a copy see the list of books in Chapter 10 or contact:

Garrett y Asociados, S.A.

Apartado 5478-1000

San José, Costa Rica

Tel: 233-2455 Fax: 222-0007

or

Garrett y Asociados

SJO 450

P.O. Box 025216

Miami, FL 33102-5216

CHAPTER THREE

Education

3.

LEARNING SPANISH

Although many of Costa Rica's well-educated people speak English, (and more than 20,000 English-speaking foreigners living permanently in Costa Rica), Spanish is the official language. Anyone who seriously plans to live or retire in Costa Rica should know Spanish — the more the better. Frankly, you will be disadvantaged, handicapped and be considered a foreigner to some degree, without Spanish. Part of the fun of living in another country is communicating with the local people, making new friends and enjoying the culture. Speaking Spanish will enable you to achieve these ends, have a more rewarding life and open the door for many new, interesting experiences. Knowing some Spanish also saves you money when you're shopping and, in some cases, keeps people from taking advantage of you.

If you take our advice and choose to study Spanish, for a modest fee you can enroll at one of Costa Rica's intensive conversational language schools. In addition to language instruction, most of these schools offer exciting field trips, interesting activities and room and board with local families—all of which are optional. Living with a family that speaks little—or preferably no—English is a wonderful way to improve your language skills, make new friends and learn about Costa Rican culture at the same time.

Spanish is not a difficult language to learn. With a little self-discipline and motivation, anyone can acquire a basic Spanish survival vocabulary of between 200 and 3000 words in a relatively short time. Many Spanish words are similar enough to English, so you can guess their meanings by just looking at them. The Spanish alphabet is almost like the English one, with a few minor exceptions. Pronunciation is easier than in English because you say words like they look like they should be said. Spanish grammar is somewhat complicated, but can be made easier if you are familiar with English grammar and find a good Spanish teacher. Practicing with native speakers improves your Spanish because you can hear how Spanish is spoken in everyday conversation. You will learn many new words and expressions not ordinarily found in your standard dictionary.

Watching Spanish television and listening to the radio and language cassettes can also improve your Spanish. We suggest that if you have little or no knowledge of spoken Spanish, you purchase the one-of-a-kind *Costa Rican Spanish Survival* book and accompanying cassette advertised in this book. It is designed especially for people planning to retire or live in Costa Rica. It makes learning easy because the student learns the natural way, by listening and repeating as a child does—without the complications of grammar. If you are interested in a more in a deeper study of Spanish, we are including a list of language schools at the end of this section. Please check first with the school of your choice for current prices.

The Spanish spoken in Costa Rica is basically standard Castillian Spanish except for one big difference confuses beginning students. Spanish has two forms for addressing a person—*usted* and *tú*. However, in Costa Rica *vos* is used instead of *tú*. The verb form used with *vos* is formed by changing the *r* at the end of a verb infinitive to *s* and adding an accent to the last syllable. This form is seldom taught because it is considered a colloquial form; used only in Central America and some parts of South America (Argentina and Uruguay). It is not found in most Spanish textbooks.

Don't worry! Once you live in Costa Rica for a while and get used to the Costa Rican way of speaking, you will learn to use the *vos* form almost automatically. If you do makes mistakes and use the *tú* form, most Costa Ricans overlook it because they know you are not a native speaker. Costa Ricans appreciate any effort you make to speak their language.

You will notice that Costa Ricans frequently use local expressions called *tiquismos*, that are not used in other Latin American countries. Some of these common expressions are: *pura vida* (fantastic, super,

LIMITED OFFER

Learn to Speak Spanish Like a Costa Rican.

Costa Rican Spanish Survival Book & Cassette

This course is a must for those who wish to get the most out of Costa Rica and be able to communicate effectively with the people. It is a process of learning by listening and repeating without boring, tiresome grammar. It has already helped thousands of people master the basics of Spanish in real life situations.

- COSTA RICAN IDIOMS

- CORRECT PRONUNCIATION

- USEFUL EVERYDAY EXPRESSIONS

- PRACTICAL VOCABULARY

- PROVEN NATURAL METHOD

- GUARANTEED RESULTS

- POCKET SIZE FOR TRAVEL

Course Material is Pocket Size -- Ideal For Travel

ORDER TODAY

ADDITIONAL CASSETTES $7.99 each
ADDITIONAL BOOKS $9.99 each

SEND CHECK OR MONEY ORDER TO:

BOOK AND CASSETTE
REGULAR $13.95 set
NOW $12.95 set
+ 3.00 handling

COSTA RICA BOOKS
P.O. BOX 1512
THOUSAND OAKS, CA
U.S.A. 91358

$15.95 set
USD

great); *tuanis* (very good); *buena nota* (good, OK); *salado* (tough luck, too bad); and many others. One saying in particular, *hijo de puta* (roughly translated as "Son of a B——"), is considered offensive and vulgar in most Spanish speaking countries, but usually not in Costa Rica. You will be shocked hearing this expressions used so frequently in everyday conversation. Even children and old women can sometimes be heard uttering this phrase. We don't encourage you to use this expression. However, be aware that it is a local custom and is usually used with no malice in mind.

For some basic Spanish phrases and more *tiquismos*, see the section titled "Important Phrases and Vocabulary."

LANGUAGE SCHOOLS

Instituto De La Lengua Española is an excellent intensive program. Six hours daily for 15 weeks for $635. Terms begin in January, May and September. Apdo. 100-2350, San José, Costa Rica. Tel: 506- 227-755; Fax: 506 -227-0211.

Forester Institute International offers a variety of classes plus field trips and the opportunity to live with a family. Prices range from $600 to $1150 depending on the program. Apdo. 6945-1000, San José, Costa Rica. Tel: 506- 225-355; Fax: 506-225-9236.

INTENSA has two, three and four week programs with home-stays available. Prices range from $260 to $545. Apdo. 8110-1000, San José. Tel: 506- 225-6009; Fax: 506 239-2225.

Centro Cultural Costarricense Norteamericana has five week courses, three hours daily for $280. Apdo. 1489-1000, San José, Costa Rica. Tel: 506-225-933; Fax: 506-224-1480.

Instituto Británico offers a three-week course, three hours a day, with field trips for $1000 includes home-stay. Apdo. 8184-1000, San José, Costa Rica. Tel: 506-234-9054; Fax: 253-1894.

Latin America Institute of Language various programs including home-stay. Some discounts. Apdo. 1001-2050, San Pedro, San José, Costa Rica. Tel. 506-225-2495; Fax: 506- 224-4665.

Institute for Central American Development Studies which teaches one-month programs, five hours a day, for $892, includes classes, lectures, field trips, and home-stay with a

Costa Rican family. Apdo. 3-2070 Sabanilla, San José, Costa Rica. Tel: 506- 225-0508; Fax: 506- 234-1337.

Academia Costarricense de Lenguaje has intensive classes and many cultural activities for $975 a month. Apdo. 336-2070, San José, Costa Rica. Tel: 506-221-1624; Fax: 506-233-8670.

Centro Panamericano de Idiomas is a new school in a beautiful rural setting. The cost is around $1000 monthly and covers instruction, home-stay and excursions. Apdo. 947-1000, San José, Costa Rica. Tel: 506- 238-061; Fax: 506- 233-8670.

Mesoamerica Language Institute gives four hours of instruction each day for $80 a week. Apdo. 300-1002, San José, Costa Rica. Tel: 506- 233-7710.

Academia Tica's various courses and home-stays cost between $120 and $180 for twenty hours of instruction. Apdo. 1294-2100, Guadalupe, San José, Costa Rica. Tel: 506-2234-0622; Fax: 805-233-9393.

DALFA Spanish School provides one month courses including excursions, cultural activities and home-stays for around $1000. Apdo. 323-1011, San Francisco de Dos Rios. Tel: 506- 226-8584.

Academia Smith Corona has various courses in downtown San José including Spanish survival courses for tourists. Apdo. 4592-1000, San José, Costa Rica. Tel: 506- 222-4637.

Centro Lingüístico Latinoamericano teaches intensive courses five hours per day for four weeks, including home-stay for $900. Apdo. 151, Alajuela, Costa Rica. Tel: 506- 241-0261.

Centro Lingüístico Conversa has an excellent conversational program at the main school in San José and another campus west of town in a rural setting. Prices vary. For more information, write to Apdo. 17-1007, Centro Colón, San José, Costa Rica. Tel: 506- 221-7649; Fax 506- 233-2418.

La Escuela D'Amore Spanish Immersion Center. This unique school, near Costa Rica's beautiful Manuel Antonio Beach on the Pacific Ocean, has small personal classes with beach lodging or home-stay available. P.O. Box 67, Quepos, Costa Rica. Tel: 506- 710-0543 U.S.A. 414-730-3151.

Instituto de Lenguaje Pura Vida in the beautiful city of Heredia offers a 20 percent discount to foreign residents of Costa Rica and their families. P.O. Box 730, Garden Grove, CA 92646. Tel: 714- 534-0125. In Costa Rica Tel: 506- 237-0387.

Simply Spanish is inexpensive and offers all levels of instruction, free social and conversational classes and home-stay. Apdo. 12471-1000, San José, Costa Rica. Tel: 506-253-0277; Fax: 506-257-2272.

Central American Institute of International Affairs (ICAI) specializes in workshops and conferences, all levels of Spanish and also offers delux tours and college credits. Apdo. 10302, San José, Costa Rica. Tel: 506-233-8571; Fax: 506-221-5238.

This list should start you on your way. Private, individualized language classes are also available. For listings look in the classified section of the Tico Times.

For a Spanish conversational club for foreigners wanting to improve their Spanish skills call 254-1433 or 235-7026. The Instituto Universal de Idiomas (Ave. 2, Calles 7/9) has an exchange club where you can practice Spanish with a native speaker in exchange for help with English (Tel: 257-0441). Centro Cultural also has free Spanish social-conversation classes through a program called "Simply Spanish" (Tel: 283-0175). The Candil Cultural center (25 meters north of the Casa Amarilla) has a language exchange program.

COSTA RICA'S INSTITUTIONS OF HIGHER LEARNING

If you who wish to continue your education, university level courses are available to foreigners in subjects such as: business, art, history, political science, biology, psychology, literature, and Spanish, as well as all other major academic areas.

Foreigners can enroll directly as special students for their first two years at the University of Costa Rica. Tuition is much lower than in most U.S. universities. Students can also audit classes for a nominal fee.

Some of the schools listed below work with U.S. universities so you can earn a degree that is recognized in the United States. You can also study to earn more credits, simply for fun to increase your general knowledge or just to stay busy. (See the next chapter for other ways to keep busy.)

- **University of Kansas Office of Studies Abroad**
  204 Lippincott Hall, Lawrence, KS 66045
- **University of California** has a one year program in conjunction

with the University of Costa Rica.
- **Associated Colleges of the Midwest,** 18 S. Michigan Ave., Suite 1010, Chicago, IL 60603 has a similar program.
- **National University of San Diego** offers a joint degree program. Apdo. 217-1017 San Jose, Costa Rica 231-5855
- **State University of New York** offers enrollment in any discipline to qualified juniors and seniors with two years of Spanish. Contact the office of International Programs L1-84, State University of New York, Albany, NY 12222.

PRIVATE UNIVERSITIES

- **Inter American University of Puerto Rico** phone.. .. 225-0979
- **University for Peace** Apdo. 199-1250, San Jose, C.R.. 249-1072
- **International University of the Americas** 233-5304
- **Autonomous University of Central America** - write UACA, Apdo. 7637-1000, San Jose, Costa Rica 441-5304

PUBLIC UNIVERSITIES

- **University of Costa Rica.** Contact Ciudad Universitaria Rodrigo Facio, San Jose, Costa Rica. 224-3660
- **State University at a Distance** (extension) 225-8788
- **Univerisad Nacional** 237-6663
- **Technical Institute of Costa Rica** 551-5333

Of course, certain requirements for these schools of higher learning must be met. Remember that private universities are generally more expensive than public universities.

OUTSTANDING PRIVATE SCHOOLS

If you have small children or teenagers you will be pleased that Costa Rica has a variety of schools to choose from. There are many public schools, numerous private bilingual schools and four English-language, or American Schools.

Costa Rica's private English-language schools are exceptional, have excellent standards and follow the U.S. school year schedule. These private schools are academically oriented and prepare students for admittance to colleges in the U.S. as well as in Costa Rica. In some ways these schools are better than similar institutions in the U.S.A., because not as many harmful distractions or bad influences exist in Costa Rica. Children also have the opportunity to learn a new language which is great value to them. The cost of some of these private schools can be more than 200 dollars per month.

Schools that follow the U.S. schedule, September to June:

Costa Rican Academy: Pre-kindergarten through grade 12. Classes taught in English, U.S. style education. Annual tuition: $1,070 pre-kindergarten, $3,130 per year for kindergarten to grade 12. Apdo. 4941-1000, San José, Costa Rica. Tel: 506- 239-0376.

Country Day School: Kindergarten through grade 12 in Escazú. Annual tuition: Pre-kindergarten $1,245; grades 1 to 12, $3,510. Apdo. 8-6170, San José, Costa Rica. Tel: 506- 228-0873; Fax: 506-228-2798.

Marian Baker School: Kindergarten through grade 12. U.S. cirriculum with classes in English. Annual tuition: Kindergarten, $2,150; preparatory to grade 6, $2,700; grades 7 - 8, $2,900; grades 9 - 12, $3,200. Apdo. 4269, San José, Costa Rica, Tel: 506- 234-4626; Fax: 506- 234-4609.

International Christan School: Pre-kindergarten through grade 12. Annual tuition: Pre-kingdergarten, $990; Preparatory and kindergarted, $1,300; Grades 1 - 6, $2,200; Grades 7 - 8, $2,300; Grades 9 - 12, $2,500. Apdo. 3512-1000, San José, Costa Rica. Tel: 225-1474.

The less expensive Bilingual private schools below, also prepare students for U.S. colleges and universities, but follow the Costa Rican academic year which begins in March and ends in November.

Anglo American School: Kindergarten through grade 6. Costs about $100 a month. Apdo. 3188-1000, San José, Costa Rica. Tel: 506-225-17-29.

Canadian International School: Pre-kindergarten through grade 2. About $100 monthly. Apdo. 622-2300. San José, Costa Rica. Tel: 506-224-2844.

Colegio Humboldt: Kindergarten through grade 12. Classes half in German, half in Spanish. Tuition is about $70 monthly. Apdo. 3749, San José, Costa Rica. Tel: 506- 232-1455.

Colegio Internacional: Pre-kindergarten through grade 10. Apdo. 963, 2050 San Pedro, Costa Rica. Tel: 506- 253-1231; Fax: 506- 225-9762.

Colegio Metodista: Kindergarten through grade 12. Classes in English and Spanish. Apdo. 931-1000, San José, Costa Rica. Tel: 506-225-0655.

Escuela Británica: Kindergarten through grade 11, classes half in English, half in Spanish. $150 per month. Apdo. 8184-1000 San José, Costa Rica. Tel: 506- 220-1719; Fax: 506-232-7833.

The European School: Pre-kindergarten through 6. Apdo. 177, Heredia, Costa Rica. Tel: 506- 237-370); Fax: 506- 231-7583.

Kiwi Kinder: Pre-school for two and a half to five-year olds. Apdo. 549-6150, Santa Ana, Costa Rica. Tel: 506-282-6512.

Liceo Franco-Costarricense: Classes in French, English and Spanish. Concepción de Tres Ríos. Tel: 506- 279-6616

Lincoln School: Pre-kindergarden through grade 12 with classes in English. Tuition about $100 monthly: Apdo. 1919, San José, Costa Rica. Tel: 506- 235-7733; Fax: 506- 236-1706.

Saint Anthony School: Pre-school through grade 6. Classes half in English, half in Spanish. Apdo. 29-2150, Moravia, Costa Rica. Tel: 235-1017.

Saint Claire: Grades 7 - 11, classes in English and in Spanish. Tuition $125 per month. Apdo. 53-2150, Moravia, Costa Rica, Tel: 506- 235-7244.

Saint Francis: Kindergarten through grade 11, classes in English and Spanish. Inquire about rates. Apdo. 4405-1000, San José Costa Rica. Tel: 506- 235-6685.

Saint Joseph's Primary School: Pre-school through grade 6, classes half in Spanish, half in English, $70 per month. Apdo. 132-2150, Moravia, Costa Rica. Tel: 506- 235-7214.

Saint Mary's: Pre- kindergarten through Grade 6, around $100 monthly. Classes in English, and Spanish. Apdo. 229-1250, Escazu, Costa Rica. Tel: 506- 228-2003.

Santa Monica Primary School: Pre-kindergarten to grade 6. Classes in English and Spanish for around $80 a month. Apdo. 53-2150, Moravia, Costa Rica. Tel: 506- 235-4119.

Saint Peter's Primary School: Pre-kindergarten to grade 6. Classes in English and Spanish for about $75 monthly. Apdo. 302-2100, Curridabat, Costa Rica. Tel: 506- 253-6869.

OTHER PRE-SCHOOLS

Centro Eductivo Las Vistas. Pre-kindergarten through grade 3. Apdo 3702, Escazú, Costa Rica. Tel: 228-1763.

El Girasol:..Ages 2 and up 232-8496

La Casa de Los Ninos Montessori:..............................228-0168

CHAPTER FOUR

Keeping Busy
in Costa Rica

SOME SOUND ADVICE

Retirement often presents new challenges for people because maybe for the first time they are confronted with having a plethora of leisure time and the problem of what to do to with it. As you will see throughout this chapter, Costa Rica is wonderful place to retire. In addition to being relatively inexpensive there are many interesting activities to choose from. As one retired American referred to his busy life in Costa Rica, "My days are so fulfilling, that each day in Costa Rica seems like a whole lifetime."

In Costa Rica you have no excuse for being bored or inactive, unless you are just plain lazy. There is some hobby or pastime for everyone regardless of age or interests. Even if you cannot pursue your favorite hobbies, you can get involved in something new and exciting. Best of all, by participating in some of the activities in this chapter, you will meet other people with common interests and cultivate new friendships in the process. Most people you meet will also be expatriates, so you probably won't need Spanish to enjoy yourself. You can even spend your time continuing your education or studying Spanish as we talked about in the last chapter.

Whatever you do, don't make the mistake of being idle. The worst thing you can do is spend all your time drinking in one of the many *gringo* hangouts in downtown San José. Over the years we have seen many fellow Americans fail to use their time constructively, and destroy their lives by becoming alcoholics while living in Costa Rica—a few even died prematurely. So, use the information we have provided in this chapter, and take advantage of all the activities Costa Rica offers. Get out and enjoy yourself!

STAY ACTIVE

ENGLISH BOOKS, MAGAZINES AND NEWSPAPERS

Books, newspapers, magazines and other printed matter in English are available at most leading bookstores, in the souvenir shops of larger hotels and at some newsstands.

Many bookstores carry a large selection of books in English. **The Bookshop** (Ave. 1, Calles 1 and 3, Tel: 221-6847) has a good selection in downtown San José. You can also find English books at **Librería Universal** (Ave. Central, Tel: 222-2222), and **Librería Lehmann** (Ave. Central, Calles 1 and 3, Tel: 223-1212).

New books in English are exhorbitantly expensive, sometimes three times the U.S. list price. So, you may be better off purchasing your books in the U.S., buying used books or going to a local library.

If you are on a tight budget, you can pick up good used books at **The Book Traders** bookstores in downtown San José (Ave. 1 between Calles 5 and 7 and above the Cine Omni on Ave. 1, Tel: 255-0508). They bill themselves as the largest used bookstore in Central America and specialize in selling and trading used books, magazines and compact disks. They also carry guide books, maps and over 30,000 books in stock.

Shakespeare & Company (Calle 3 between Ave. 5 and 7, Tel: 233-4995) is a new bookstore featuring a wide selection of English language books. **Gambit** (Calle 37, Ave. 3, Tel: 224-5170) is a small bookstore in the suburb of Los Yoses. **The Apple Bookstore,** in the Yohan Shopping Center, also stocks English books. **Stauter** (Plaza del Sol Shopping Center, Tel: 234-2257) and **The Bookstop** (Ave. 3, Calles 19 and 21, Tel: 223-5300) round out the list of bookstores selling English language books.

Three major libraries in the San José area have large collections of English language books and magazines.

The place to go for the best selection of books is the **Mark Twain Library** at the North American–Central American Culture Institute, commonly known as the **Centro Cultural**. You can browse all day or check out books. They also have nearly one hundred English magazines to choose from. Call 253-5783 for more information.

The **National Library**, near downtown San José, is not a browsing library but has a large selection of novels and magazines in English. You have to use the card catalog to select your book and then request it at the front desk.

Also, the **University of Costa Rica Library** has some materials in English.

There is no problem obtaining copies of *Miami Herald, New York Times, Time* or *Newsweek* in Costa Rica. As we mentioned, you can pick up most English newspapers and magazines at local newsstands, hotels and some bookstores. You can also arrange to have many of the newspapers we mention in this section delivered to your home or office the same day they are published by calling **Agencia de Publicaciones** at 259-5555, 259-5656, or 259-0812.

OTHER ENGLISH LANGUAGE PUBLICATIONS AVAILABLE:
* *Barron's*
* *International Herald Tribune*
* *Sporting News*
* *Sports Illustrated*
* *USA Today*
* *Wall Street Journal*
* *Washington Post*

The largest English newspaper published in Central America, *The Tico Times*, is available almost everywhere. Reading it is an excellent way to keep up with local Costa Rican and Central American news in general. Car sales, cultural activities and other useful information can also be found in this newspaper. By looking in the personals in the classified ads you can even find companionship. Pick up a copy as soon as you arrive. It comes out every Friday.

To subscribe to the *Tico Times* (if you live in the U.S.) write Dept. 717, P.O. Box 025216, Miami, FL 33102. If you live in Costa Rica: Apdo. 4362, San José, Costa Rica.

Another excellent newspaper, *Costa Rica Today,* made its debut a couple of years ago. This paper is more for tourists than the *Tico Times* and doesn't carry much news or have much sensationalism like its counterpart. To subscribe write: *Costa Rica Today* 117, P.O. Box 0025216, Miami FL 33102. There is no need to subscribe locally since you can this paper almost anywhere. It comes out on Thursdays.

TELEVISION AND RADIO

As in the United States, Costa Rica has satellite cable television. A variety of American television channels provide viewing and entertainment at a low cost from any of the companies listed below. A new cable company, TV America, offers both the ABC and CBS networks for the first time in Costa Rica. If you don't want to subscribe to cable TV and have a home where you can install your own satellite dish, contact, Orbita, S.A.. A limited number of American channels are available on UHF by purchasing a UHF antenna.

Most radio stations play primarily Latin music, but others play music more familiar to Americans.

To order cablevision call one of these numbers.

TV AMERICA (CBS & ABC) 226-9333, 226-9092

CABLE COLOR .... 231-3838, 231-2811 or 231-3939

SUPER CANAL .... 232-2244 or 442-1910

CABLE TICA .... 718-8614 or 254-8858

CLUB CABLE .... 551-3886 or 238-1756

CHANNEL 19, Master Television

ORBITA, S.A. for satellite dishes .... 223-1868; Fax 255-0652

VIDEO RENTALS

Video buffs will be happy that many video rental shops do business in the San José area. For a small initial fee you can acquire a membership at one of these stores and enjoy many privileges. Most movies you rent are in English with Spanish subtitles.

Video Flash (Curridabat) 253-7379
Video de las Américas (two locations) 253-6545, 257-0303
Video Express (have delivery and pick up service)..... 221-3466
Video Movies (Curridabat).. 253-5034
Hollywood Video Club (two locations)...... 225-0630, 227-4869
Home Movie 2000 231-4352
See the phone book for additional listings.

SHOPPING

One way to keep active is to go shopping. Although Costa Rica is not as commercialized as the U.S., you can still spend your free time doing  some serious shopping, browsing or just window shopping.

Because of the large number of U.S. and Canadian citizens living in Costa Rica, and a growing number of Costa Ricans exposed to U.S. culture by cable TV and visiting the states, there has been an influx of American products. The only problem is that many of these goods are more expensive in Costa Rica because of import duties.

Everyday more and more imported goods from the U.S. are available in Costa Rica. Imported brand name cosmetics, stylish clothing, appliances and some foods, can now be found in many stores in San José, and other areas catering to foreigners.

A number of new stores and shopping centers in or near San José now sell imported items. In downtown San José a few specialty shops and a couple of department stores sell American-style clothing and other imported goods.

Plaza del Sol, Costa Rica's first U.S.-style mall, is about five minutes east of San José in Curridabat. A mall is also found at the **Plaza Mayor Shopping Center** in Rohrmoser.

In the suburb of Escazú, home of many foreigners and well-to-do Costa Ricans, a number of U.S.-style mini-malls have sprung up. Most of these newer stores have products that foreigners look for.

There is a new, large shopping mall, **El Centro Comercial Multiplaza** west of Escazú. This complex houses Costa Rica's largest mall and shopping center.

Despite the availability of many new products, and the growing number of malls, mini-malls and specialty shops, shopping in Costa Rica still leaves a lot to be desired if you are used to the U.S. or Canada. Don't expect U.S. style shopping in Costa Rica.

As we mention in Chapter 9, if you live in Costa Rica, you have to substitute many local products for items you ordinarily use and do without some things. This is easy because of the variety of similar products available in Costa Rica. However, if you must have products from the states, you can go to the U.S. every few months—as many foreigners and wealthy Costa Ricans do— to stock up on canned goods and other non-perishable foods, clothing, sundries and cosmetics. We know of one American retiree who goes to Miami every three or four months to buy all the goodies he can't find in Costa Rica. These frequent trips to the states are unecessary if you want to learn to make do with the local products.

COSTA RICAN PASTIMES

Costa Rica has a wealth of indoor and outdoor activities designed for everyone regardless of sex, age, personal taste or budget. All of us—Costa Ricans, tourists and foreign residents—can participate in river rafting (some of the world's best), camping, walking groups, dancing, racketball, weight lifting, tennis, baseball, soccer, swimming and surfing, bowling, jogging, bicycling, horseback riding, and sailing. There are also plays, ceramics classes, movies, bridge, art galleries, social clubs, museums, parks, zoos and more. Dedicated couch-potatoes can even stretch out and admire the lovely landscape or work on improving their suntans. There is something for everyone and everything for someone—so enjoy.

Check the activities section of the *Tico Times*, or *Costa Rica Today*.

If you wish to join a private athletic club, country club or gym we suggest:

The Indoor Club Curridabat	225-9344
The Spa Corobicí	232-8122
Costa Rican Tennis Club	232-1266
Costa Rican Country Club in Escazú	228-9333
Cariari Country Club (golf)	239-2455

Bello Horizonte Country Club 228-0924
Costa Rica Yacht Club 223-4224
Spa Cariari Hotel 239-0022
Club Olímpico 228-5051

FISHING IN COSTA RICA

People who enjoy spending their leisure time fishing find Costa Rica the perfect place to live. Costa Rica has some of the world's best sportfishing. Take your choice. Fish either the Caribbean or the Pacific, but don't forget those gentle miles of meandering rivers or the fresh water lakes. Lake Arenal is famous for its *guapote* trout. More important, most fishing areas are only a few hours driving time from anywhere in Costa Rica.

Costa Rica is considered to be one of the best year-round fishing areas in the world. The fishing is outstanding almost all of the time and almost everywhere in Costa Rica. Even when it rains it isn't so bad since your chances of hooking some excellent sport fish are very good. When it comes to sailfish, tarpon or snook, no place is better.

If you are really hooked on fishing, and want to keep up with the local fishing scene, pick up a copy of the *Tico Times* or *Costa Rica Today*. Both papers have excellent weekly fishing columns. The column in *Costa Rica Today* is written by legendary fishing columnist Jerry Ruhlow. He is also the editor of the newly published newsletter, *Costa Rica Outdoors*, which features articles on fishing and other outdoor sports.

For the most up-to-date fishing information, contact **American Fishing Services**. Tell them what fish you want to catch and they will help you. Their office is in the Hotel Del Rey in downtown San José, one block south of Morazán Park. For more information call or fax and ask to speak to Richard Krug, the other local fishing expert and fishing columnist for the *Tico Times*, at Tel: 011-506-221-7272 or Fax: 011-506-221-0096.

Listed below are some of the better fishing camps all of which have great accommodations and experienced English-speaking fishing guides.

Carribbean Fishing:
Tortuga Lodge 223-0333

Parismina Tarpon Rancho 235-7766
Casamar 441-2820
Río Colorado .... 232-4063 or 232-8610

Pacific Fishing:
Flamingo Bay Pacific Charters .... 680-0444 or 680-0620
Bahía Pez Vela: (Ocotal) .... 221-1586 or 670-0129
Papagayo Excursions 680-0859
Oasis del Pacífico (Nicoya) 661-1555
Sports Fishing Quepos 233-9135
Costa Rican Dreams (Quepos) 777-0593
Tango Mar (Tambor) 661-2798
Golfito Sports Fishing 775-0353
Reel'n Release Sportfishing (Dominical) 771-1903
Blue Marlin Fishing (Flamingo Beach) 654-4043

Freshwater Trout Fishing:
Adventuras Tilarán (Arenal) 695-5008
Finca Zacatecales 771-1732

Nearly all of these fishing camps and lodges have overnight accommodations which include meals. Fishing equipment and boats are also provided.

For the listing of other fishing camps and tours, read the *Tico Times* and *Costa Rica Today* or consult a local travel agency.

COSTA RICA'S PRISTINE BEACHES

Unlike many resort areas in Mexico and Latin America, Costa Rica's beautiful tropical beaches and 767 miles of coastline are virtually unspoiled. Water temperatures are very warm so you can stay in all day.

Moving from north to south along the west coast, are many white and dark sand beaches and numerous resorts.

In the Guanacaste area the following beaches are found: Playa Naranjo, Playa Panama, Playa Hermosa, Playa del Coco (a favorite *gringo* hangout) Ocotal, Bahía Pez Vela, Playa Protrero, Playa Flamingo, Playa Brasilito, Conchal, Playa Grande, Playa Tamarindo, Playa Avellana, and Playa Junquillal.

As we move south many beaches are scattered along the coast of the Nicoya Peninsula: Playa Azul, Playa Nosara, Playa Samara, Playa Carrillo, Playa Coyote. Playa Montezuma near the eastern tip of Nicoya, is a nice beach.

Moving even farther south along the Pacific Coast are: Puntarenas (Costa Rica's main port), Boca Barranca (good surfing beach), Mata Limón, Playa Tivives, Playa Tarcoles, Playa Escondido, Playa Herradura, Playa Jacó, Playa Hermosa, Esterillos, Quepos, Manuel Antonio (considered by many to be the most beautiful beach in Costa Rica), Playa Dominical and the beaches around the town of Uvita.

On the Atlantic side are: Playa Bonita (Portete), Punta Cahuita (beautiful beach), Puerto Viejo, Playa Uva and Playa Manzanillo.

Please see the map in the front of this book to locate some of the beaches we mention.

NATIONAL PARKS FOR NATURE LOVERS

Costa Ricans take pride in their extensive national park system. Since Costa Rica is rich  not only in natural beauty but in all varietiesof wild life, Costa Ricans have set aside 20 percent of their territory and established 36 national parks and preserves to protect the flora and fauna of their country.

Costa Rica's parks are in every region of the country with some more accessible than others. The variety of birds, butterflies, amphibians, mammals, trees and flowers has to be seen to be believed.

Additional information and a list of parks may be obtained by calling 233-5673, 233-5284 or 233-4160. Most hotels and tourist information centers can be helpful to nature lovers. Please note: since reserves are more strictly protected than parks, a permit is usually necessary. Foreigners pay about $15 admission and Costa Ricans and residents $1.50 to enter Costa Ricas parks. At the same time, officials have set limits on the number of visitors permitted inside the most popular parks—Manuel Antonio, Poás, Irazú, Tortuguero and Carara Biological Reserve—at one time.

MAKING NEW FRIENDS IN COSTA RICA

You should have no problem making new friends in Costa Rica, but might have some difficulty meeting Costa Ricans if you speak little or no Spanish. You will be surprised how many Costa Ricans speak some English and are dying for the chance to perfect their English language skills while you work on your Spanish. Perhaps you can find someone to exchange language lessons with. This is a good way to make new acquaintances and learn how Spanish is really spoken.

You most certainly will find it easier to meet fellow Americans in Costa Rica than in the U.S., because Americans living abroad tend to gravitate toward each other. Newcomers only have to find an enclave of fellow countrymen and they can make many new friends. You can't help bumping into other Americans since Costa Rica is such a small country (there are over 20,000 gringos living there permanently). This is especially true if you live in one of the areas where many North Americans reside, like Escazú or Rohrmoser. Another good way of contacting other foreign residents is by participating in some of the activities listed in the weekly editions of the, *Tico Times* and *Costa Rica Today*. These newspapers serve as a vital link in the foreign community, or "*Gringo* Grapevine", and help put you in touch with the whole network of expatriates and the services they offer.

At any of the local *gringo* watering holes in downtown San José, such as Nashville South, Tiny's Tropical Sports Bar or the Piano Blanco Bar, you can watch live sporting events from the U.S. on cable T.V. or simply shoot the breeze with your compatriots. Many Americans also congregate at the Plaza de La Cultura and at McDonald's across the street, where they linger over coffee every morning and watch the beautiful women pass by.

You have no reason to be lonely unless you want to be. Just be yourself and you will find Costa Rica is just the place for you. Oh yes, we might add that there are poetry readings, art and sculpture exhibitions as well as other activities where people can easily socialize. The American Costa Rican Cultural Center has many events where you can also make new acquaintances.

CLUBS AND ORGANIZATIONS :

Amnesty International...253-5348

American Legion Post (Escazú)............................228-1740
American Poker Club..223-4331
Democrats Abroad..233-3896
Disabled American Veterns...............................443-2508
Investment Club of Costa Rica..........................240-2240
Kiwanas Club...438-0038
National Bridge Association..............................253-2762
Newcomers' Club...228-6347
Personal Computer Club....................................249-1806
Republicans Abroad...276-7250
Rotary Club...222-0993
Square Dance Club...253-5527
Vía Holística(Health and Personal Awareness).............282-6107
Women's Club of Costa Rica...............................236-0525

* For a complete listing of clubs and related activities, look under
  the weekly "What's Doing" section in the *Tico Times*, or in the
  Calendar of Events section in, *Costa Rica Today*.

FINDING LOVE AND PERMANENT COMPANIONSHIP

If you are looking for someone for romance, Costa Rica might just be the right place for you.

Ladies, regardless of age, you will find gentleman admirers if you so desire. Due to *machismo* Costa Rican men are more flirtatious and aggressive than North American men. Most Costa Rican men think foreign women have looser morals and are easier conquests than *ticas* (Costa Rican women). So, be careful to take time to develop a long-term, meaningful relationship and don't rush things.

Men of any age, will have no problem meeting Costa Rican women. The women in Costa Rica seem to like older, more experienced men. It is not unusual to see a wife who is ten to twenty younger than her spouse. This practice may be frowned on in some countries but is accepted in Costa Rica. Many retirees we know claim to feel rejuvenated and to have a new lease on life after becoming involved with younger women.

Costa Rican women have an unparalleledreputation as being the most beautiful, flirtatious, and accessible women in Latin America—including Brazil. The ladies of Costa Rica are more warm-hearted and eternally devoted than their North American counterparts. They consider you a joy. One retiree we know boasts, "The women here really know how to treat you like a king!"

A man doesn't even have to be rich to meet women—an $800 Social Security check translates to a millionaire's pay in Costa Rica.

No wonder Costa Rican women are highly sought by foreign men. However, before becoming involved with a Costa Rican woman, you should realize the many cultural differences that can lead to all sorts of problems, especially if you don't speak Spanish fluently.

Generally, Latin women are more jealous and possessive than American women, and tend not to understand our ways unless they have lived in the United States. Also, be aware that because of their comparative wealth, most Americans, especially the elderly, are considered prime targets for some unscrupulous Latin females.

As we alluded to at the end of the first chapter, in some cases there is another bad side of marrying a Costa Rican woman in that you can end up supporting her whole family either directly or indirectly as many foreigners complain. There is a book titled, "Happy Aging With Costa Rican Women - The Other Costa Rica" by James Y. Kennedy (published by Box Canyon Books). It tells all about the trials and tribulations and experiences many gringos have with Costa Rican women.

We advise you to give any relationship time and make sure a woman is sincerely interested in you and not just your money—you will save yourself a lot of grief and heartache in the long run. Since prostitution is legal and available to men of all ages, be careful of the ladies of ill-repute. Many foreigners after inviting one of these females to spend the night, wake up the next day without the woman and minus wallets and other valuables.

Most single men can avoid getting involved with gold diggers, prostitutes, or other troublesome women if they know where to look for good women. The personals section of the Tico Times is an excellent place to advertise for companionship. It is relatively inexpensive and many Costa Rican women read this section each week. Check out the current or past issues of the Tico Times for ideas on how to write one of these ads.

One American we know ran an ad in the *Tico Times* and the local Spanish newspapers and ended up screening hundreds of women before finding his ideal mate. As far as we know he is still happily married.

Taking classes at the university is another way to meet quality women. The university in San Pedro is full of beautiful well-educated females. Cafés, restaurants, bars and other places around the university are good places to meet women.

Finally, if you have Costa Rican friends, they will usually be able introduce you to someone worthwhile.

NIGHTLIFE AND ENTERTAINMENT

There are countless open air restaurants, bars, dance halls and discotheques all over San José and in most other parts of the country. Costa Ricans love to party and dance. No doubt when you have lived in the country for a while, you will be bitten by the dance bug. If you want to learn to dance like a Costa Rican, call the Costa Rican Latin dance Academy at 221-1624 or 233- 8914, for lessons.

Once you have mastered the basic dance steps of Latin dancing, put on your best pair of dancing shoes and go to **El Gran Parqueo** dance hall in the suburb of San Rafael de Desamparados. The dance floor is huge and the place really fills up on the weekends. **Los Higuerones**, next door, is another good place to dance the night away.

San José's many discotheques and dance halls play music for all tastes until the wee hours of the morning; admission is inexpensive or free. International liquors and cocktails, as well as all local beers and beverages are served. Also, keep in mind that many of these clubs serve food and the traditional heaping plates of delicious local appetizers or hôrs d'oeuvres, called *Bocas*.

Most of these establishments are quiet by day and artistically decorated. Many have adjoining restaurants, live music or a disc jockey and well-lighted dance floors.

If you want something more romantic, the famous mariachis at **La Esmeralda** will serenade you with their guitars, trumpets and violins.

This bar doesn't start jumping until 10 p.m. and stays open until 5 a.m. The front of the bar is open and faces Avenida 2, creating a unique atmosphere. If rock and roll music is more to your liking, try the **Rock Café** on Paseo Colón. **Rockola's** at the Los Yoses shopping center plays tunes from the 60s and 70s. Rock posters and LPs adorn the walls of this bar. Bohemian types should check out **El Cuartel de La Boca del Monte**. Old hippies and Costa Rican yuppies mingle there.

For lovers of jazz there are several good clubs in the San José area. The **Shakespeare Bar**, next to the Sala Garbo, offers nice mellow jazz piano several nights each week. **The Emilia Romagna Jazz Club** presents weekly concerts.

If you like the university atmosphere, the college crowd and bar -hopping, then the suburb of **San Pedro** is just the place for you. The area around the university is full of college type hangouts. Most of these places are full any night of the week. There is some entertainment here for everyone. Check out **TX Antojería Bar** if you like loud music. **Baleares** offers different types of music. Patrons can also play darts, backgammon, chess and a variety of other board games when there is no live music. **La Villa** is the perfect place to go if you are the hip-intellectual type.

For those of you who don't like loud music, sports bars, large crowds or a boisterous atmosphere, some more sedate establishments let you relax with friends and enjoy conversation.

Most hotels bars have a laid-back ambience. **The Hotel Grano de Oro** has a lovely patio where you may sit and nurse your favorite beverage. **The Amstel Hotel Lounge** is another quiet place to retreat. For the best free *bocas* in Costa Rica, we suggest you try the **Yugo de Oro**.

WHERE TO GO FOR NIGHTLIFE AND ENTERTAINMENT

Antojitos .... Good Mexican food
Bar Mexico .... Live music
Chelles .... People watching hangout
Chelles Taberna .... Another people watching hangout.
Classic Rock & Roll Bar .... Good Rock
Cocoloco .... Large disco at El Pueblo Shopping Center
Dennies .... Quiet bar & restaurant, live music
Infinito .... Another disco at El Pueblo Shopping Center

Mirador Ram Luna .... Family style, jukebox, dancing
Soda La Perla .... Meeting place
Salsa 54 .... Great dancing downtown
Túnel del Tiempo .... More dancing downtown
La Plaza .... Elegant with large dance floor
Cocodrilo .... In San Pedro, fun
Los Tunas .... Restaurant, bar, discotheque
Bar Atlas .... Discotheque, happy hour
Bromelia's Cafe and Grill ...... Live cool jazz and happy hour
Friday's .... In San Pedro, great American style food

THE *GRINGO* BAR SCENE

As we wrote earlier, there are a several *gringo* bars,
which cater almost exclusively to expatriates, in downtown
San José or nearby. Although we don't recommend hanging
out at these places 24-hours a day, there is no better way to
hear stories about life in the tropics, keep up on local gossip,
meet some colorful local characters and gather tips about
living in Costa Rica while you sip your favorite beverage.
   One of our favorite watering holes is **Tiny's Tropical
Sports Bar**. It is probably San José's best sports bar and is packed
during any major sporting event. You should check out their annual
Super Bowl and Saint Patrick's day parties. They have large color
televisions for such occasions.
   Lucky's Piano Bar next door to Hotel Balmoral, is a people-
watching bar because its large plate glass window provides a view of
busy Avenida Central.
   Nashville South is a country western bar with an interesting
clientele and western decor.
   Another *gringo* hangout is the bar at the **Dunn Inn Hotel**. You can
always meet expatriates here. The owner, Pat "Tex" Dunn used to run
Nashville South and a couple of other *gringo* bars. He is a congenial
man who can provide you with information about living in Costa Rica.
Risas is a quaint bar with a low ceiling and mirrored walls in downtown
San José. The owners are from the U.S. and the clientele is mostly
Costa Rican yuppies and *gringos*. By the way, they serve great food.
Try some of their sandwiches.
   Five minutes from downtown, in the suburb of Los Yoses, you will
find one of the area's hottest new bars—**Catástrofe** (Catastrophe).
This bar used to be run by a long-time Costa Rican character and
legend, the late Jimmy Adams. Another great *gringo* spot is the *Blue*

Marlin Bar in the Hotel Del Rey. This bar is frequented by sport enthusiasts. You'll hear a bit of friendly boasting and some tall fish tales at this unique bar. If you want to make some acquaintances, this bar is worth visiting.

The dingy **New York Bar, Happy Days** and **The Park Hotel Bar**, are other bars in downtown San José where you can find Americans and Canadians, some locals and many "Ladies of the night." Speaking of night clubs, at the **Key Largo**, across from Morazán Park in a beautiful, old mansion, you can hear live music nightly and find female companionship, if you so desire. This bar generally fills up around 10:00 p.m.

The **American Bar**, in Escazú is another bar where many *gringos* hang out.

FULL SERVICE COCKTAIL BARS

Most bars open at 11 a.m. and close at 2 a.m—7 days per week. Some have happy hours.

Promesas .... Avenida Central. Good for people watching.
Charleston .... Nice ambience.
Las Yuntas .... Great snacks with each drink.
Hotel Corobicí.. Good bar.
Holiday Inn .... Across from Morazán Park.
Hotel Irazú .... Two drinks for one on Fridays.
La Soda Tapia................. Nice place across from Sabana Park.
Hotel Balmoral .... Nice quiet bar.
Yesterday's .... Downtown San José.
Soda Palace .... Open 24 hours, across from Central Park.
Besito's Bar .... Good music on tape and TV.
Marley's .... Ave. 1--downtown.
Taberna Cayuco .... Calle 11, Ave. 1& 3, X-rated movies.
Bar EL Higueron .... In San Pedro.
Josephine's .... Live dance shows and good nightclub.
Rio .... Has a nice outdoor area and porch.
Cus bar .... Ave. Central caters to the younger set.
Sand Bar .... Behind Los Antojitos in Los Yoses.

GAMBLING

Costa Rica has about twenty casinos most in the San José area and a few at various beach resorts. Rules are slightly different than in the U.S.A. or Europe, but gambling is fun to learn the Costa Rican way. There are four legal casino games. Rummy, a variation of black jack or 21, is the most popular of these casino games. Craps, roulette (played lottery style rather than with a wheel) and *tute* a type of poker played against the house. Slot machines and sports betting are illegal and not permitted. Most casinos give free drinks while you play and are open from 6 p.m. to 3 or 4 a.m. The Gran Hotel Costa Rica has 24-hour gambling.

WHERE TO GO:
- San José Palacio (The newest, largest and best casino in the country)
- Hotel Cariari
- Holiday Inn (Check out the panoramic view of San José)
- Balmoral Hotel
- Hotel Corobicí
- Hotel Irazú
- Hotel Presidente
- Club Triángulo
- Hotel Sheraton Herradura
- Hotel Costa Rica
- Le Chambord Restaurant
- Royal Garden
- Club Colonial
- Hotel Del Rey (A centrally located *gringo* hangout)

The most popular form of gambling in Costa Rica is the national lottery or *lotería*. This game of chance is played a couple of times each week. You can purchase a whole sheet of tickets or a fraction of a ticket from any street venor. A substantial amount of money may be won if you have a winning ticket. If you are lucky enough to win the huge, annual Christmas Lottery, or *Gordo Navideño*, you will become very rich and probably set up for life. To find the results of the lottery, look in the local newspaper.

There is also an instant winner lottery similar to that played in the U.S., called *raspa*. In this game you scrape off an area on the ticket with a coin to see if you have matching symbols or numbers.

You can now bet on racehorses in Costa Rica. The Hipódromo del Sol racetrack, in San Rafael de Ojo de Agua, opened in the spring of 1994. There are off-track betting facilities in some hotels. A future plan is to show races on closed circuit television.

MOVIES AND THEATERS

There are movie theaters all over the San José area and in other large cities. Most of these theaters show first-run movies usually a month or two after they first screen in the United States. About 40 percent of all current hit movies shown in the United States make their way to Costa Rica sooner or later. You shouldn't worry about understanding these movies since they are all in English with Spanish subtitles. You can read  the local newspapers to see what movies are currently playing. At present, admission is a little over two dollars.

San José is purported to have more theatres and theater companies per capita than any other city in the world. Most live plays are in Spanish but there are occasional plays in English at the North American Cultural Center. However, by going to plays presented in Spanish, you can improve your language skills. Current stage plays are also listed in the activities section of local newspapers.

MOVIES (CINES)

Cine Bellavista 221-0909
   Ave. Central, Calles 17 & 19

Cine California... 221-4738
   Calle 23, Ave. 1

Cine Capri 223-0264
   Ave. Central, Calles 9 & 1

Cine Magaly 223-0085
   Calle 23, Ave. Central & 1

Cine Omni 221-7903
    Behind Macdonald's and the Plaza de la Cultura

Cine Rex 221-0041
    Calle Central, Avenida 6 & 8

Cine Universal 221-5241
    Paseo Colón, Calle 26 & 28

Cine Colón 221-4517
    Centro Colón Building

Sala Garbo 222-1034
    100 meters south of Pizza Hut Paseo Colón

Cine Variedades 222-6104
    Ave. Central & 1 Calle 5

Cine Colonial 1 & 2...289-9000
    Centro Comercial Escazú

Four movie theaters are scheduled to open in the new San Pedro
Mall.

THEATERS (TEATROS) IN AND AROUND SAN JOSE

Teatro La Comedia 255-3255
    Next to Más por Menos Market on Ave. Central

Teatro Laurence Olivier... 222-1034
    Ave. 2, Calle 28

Teatro Arlequin 222-0792
    Calle 13, Ave. Central

Sala J. Vargas Calvo... 222-1875
    Calles 3 & 5, Ave. 2

Teatro del Angel.. 222-8258
    Ave. Central & Plaza de la Democracia

Teatro Melico Salazar 221-4952
    Ave. 2, Calle Central

Teatro de La Aduana 223-4563
    Calle 25, Avenidas 3 & 5

Teatro Capra 234-2866
    Calles 29 & 33, Ave. 1

Teatro Chaplin 223-2919
    Paseo de Los Estudiantes

Teatro Calle 15 222-6626
    Calle 15, Avenida 2

Teatro Máscara 255-4250
    Calle 13, Avenidas 2 & 4

Teatro Nacional... 221-5341
    Ave. 2, Calles 3 & 5

Teatro Tiempo 222-0792
    Ave. Central & 2, Calle 13

Facultad de Bellas Arles
    University of Costa Rica

Vibrant downtown San José.

COSTA RICAN SCENES

The end of another day in paradise.

Costa Rica offers something for everyone. Truly, a land worth exploring: from its beautiful tropical beaches to its majestic alpine-like mountains.

Top: This colorful macaw is a prime example of the local fauna.

Center: Nature's wonders abound in Costa Rica.

Bottom: River rafting is one of the many outdoor activities Costa Rica has to offer.

Top: Lake Arenal in all its splendor.

Center: One of the country's many spectacular beaches.

Bottom: Costa Rica is a sportfisherman's paradise.

Top: Costa Rica's fertile soil and climate produce a phenomenon called, "A living fence."

Center: Costa Rica's hardwood furniture.

Bottom: A beautiful hybiscus.

Photographs courtesy of S. Miller, "Costa Rican Outlook."

CHAPTER FIVE

Getting Around

AIR TRAVEL TO, IN AND AROUND COSTA RICA

Most direct flights through Miami cost less, however there are flights from your home city to San José by way of Los Angeles, Houston, New Orleans, or Panama. The airlines offering service from the United States to San José, Costa Rica are Aviateca, Sasha, Continental, Mexicana, TACA, American, United, Aero Costa Rica (1-800-237-6274) and LACSA Costa Rica's national airline. Lacsa's toll-free number is 1-800-225-2272 in the U.S.A. and 1-800-663-2444 in Canada.

Some airline tickets are good for a year, but you need permission from the Costa Rican Immigration Department to stay in the country longer than 90 days, unless you are a Costa Rican resident or *pensionado*. Most airlines offer excursion rates and three-or-four week packages. Others, especially Canadian airlines, offer special group and charter rates. Fares are subject to availability, change and restrictions including advanced purchase requirements, minimum stops or cancellation penalties. Remember, the main tourist season in Costa Rica runs from about Thanksgiving to Easter. This period approximately coincides with local vacations so it is hard to find available space at this time off year. If you are planning to travel to or from

LACSA -
COSTA RICA'S AIRLINE

Costa Rica during December you may have to buy a ticket months in advance because of the Christmas holidays. However, if you get into a jam you can sometimes find space on a flight via Panama.

Finally, if you plan to travel or explore South America from Costa Rica, you can usually save money by flying to Miami and then buying a round-trip ticket to your destination. For instance, a one-way ticket from San José to Buenos Aires, Argentina can cost more than a round trip ticket from Miami to Buenos Aires. So, check prices from Miami to other Latin American destinations.

Costa Rica Travel Exchange (1-800-256-0124) and **About Costa Rica** (1-800-423-9731) are full-service U.S. tour operators who offer low fares to Costa Rica.

INTERNATIONAL AIRLINES LOCATED IN SAN JOSE, COSTA RICA

Areolíneas Argentinas, Ave. 1 Calle 3-5 222-1332
American Airlines La Sabana 222-5655
Avianca/SAM, Ave. 5 Calle 1 221-3311
Continental, Juan Santamaria Airport 233-0266
COPA, Ave. 5 Calle 1 222-7033
Iberia, Ave. 2-4 Calle 1 221-3311
KLM 220-4141
LACSA, La Uruca 231-0033
Mexicana 222-1711
Nica 222-1744
Sasha, Ave. 5 Calle 1-3 221-5774
TACA 222-1710
United 220-4844

DOMESTIC AIRLINES

Smaller domestic airlines like SANSA or chartered, called air taxis are used for flights within the country. The latter can cost up to a few hundred dollars an hour. SANSA, the national airline, is more reasonably priced ($15 to $30, depending on your destination). SANSA flies to the beach cities of Golfito, Quepos, Barra del Colorado, Samara, Nosara, and Tamarindo. We recommend purchasing your tickets in advance, especially during the heavy tourist season (December to May.) These flights get you to your designation quickly and economically, save you time and give you the thrill of viewing Costa Rica's spectacular landscape from above.

The SANSA office is on Paseo Colón and Calle 24. Telephone 233-5330 for flight times and reservations. Some travel agencies in San José also make reservations.

AIR TAXIS

AVIONES TAXI AEREO S.A. .... 441-1626 or 441-2062
TAXI AEREO CENTRO AMERICANO S.A. 232-1317 or 232-1438
TRAVELAIR .... 332-7883 or 320-3054
Also look in the yellow pages under "Taxis Aereos."

TRAVELING BY BUS IN COSTA RICA

As you already know, bus fares in San José and to surrounding suburbs are very cheap. Also, for a very low cost ($2– $6, or about $1 per hour of driving time) you can take a bus to almost anywhere in the country. Most Costa Ricans don't own cars, so they depend on buses for traveling to other parts of the country.   Riding a bus provides the perfect opportunity to get to know people on a personal basis, see the lovely countryside and learn something about the country and the culture. Most buses used for these longer trips are modern, and very comfortable. Unlike some parts of Latin America, Costa Rica's buses are not filled with chickens and other small animals and NO standing is allowed. Buses are crowded on weekends and holidays, so buy your tickets in advance or get to the station early. Be sure to check for schedule changes.

Alajuela (a bus every 20 minutes or so) Ave. 2,
    Calle 12 and 14 222-5325
Cartago (a bus every 10 minutes) Calle 13,
    Central Ave. 2 233-5350
Golfito (get tickets in advance) Ave. 18, Calle 2 and 4 221-4214
Heredia (a bus every 5 minutes) Calle 1, Ave. 7 and 9 233-8392
Liberia (get tickets in advance) Calle 14, Ave. 1 and 3 222-1650
Limón (Hourly, 6 a.m. to 6 p.m., get tickets in advance on holidays)
Ave. 3, Calle 19 and 21 223-7811
Nicoya (get tickets in advance) Calle 14, Ave. 3 and 5 222-2750
Puntarenas (every 30 minutes. Be early on holidays) Calle12, Ave.
7and 9 222-0064
Quepos (get tickets in advance inside the market)
    Coca Cola Terminal 223-5567

San Carlos (a bus every hour) Coca Cola Terminal 255-4318
Santa Cruz Calle 14, Ave.1 and 3. 221-7202
San Isidro del General (get tickets in advance)
    Calle 16, Ave. 1 and 3 .... 223-3577, 223-0681, 222-2422
Sarchí (ride the NARANJO BUS, every hour)
    Calle 16, Ave. 1 and 3 441-3781
Southern Border (Paso Canoas, leaves daily)
    Ave. 18, Calle 2 and 4 223-7685
Tilarán - (leaves daily) Calle 14, Ave. 9 and 11 222-3854
Turrialba Calle 13, Ave. 6 and 8 556-0073

* If your destination is not listed check with a local travel agency, the tourist office under the Plaza de La Cultura in downtown San José, or some knowledgable person who is familiar with bus schedules and knows the different bus stops.

BUS TRAVEL TO AND FROM COSTA RICA

If you want to travel to Guatemala, Panama or other Central American countries, you can use the bus services listed. Those wanting to live in Costa Rica permanently without being legal residents can take a bus to Panama or Nicaragua, return to Costa Rica after 72 hours, and thus renew your papers so you can remain legally in the country for another 90 days. Many foreigners, living as perpetual tourists in Costa Rica, go through this procedure every few months in order to avoid immigration hassles. Note: This is illegal and we do **not** recommend it.

From time to time the immigration department asks to see a return ticket before extending tourist cards. So, it is a good idea to buy an inexpensive bus ticket to a neighboring country to prove you can leave the country.

San José to Panama City leaves daily at 10 p.m. from Avenida 4 between Calles 9 and 11. The 542 mile journey takes twenty hours. Tel: 221-8954.

San José to David (Panama) leaves daily at 7:30 a.m. from Avenida 18 between Calles 2 and 4. It makes the 240 mile trip in 9 hours. Tel: 221-421).

San José to Managua, Nicaragua leaves at 7 a.m. The 270 mile trip takes about 11 hours. Tel: 221-8954 or 223-1464.

San José to Guatemala leaves daily at 7:30 a.m. from Avenida 4 between Calles 9 and 11. This trip takes 2-1/2 days. Tel: 221-8954.

TRAVELING BY TRAIN

Unfortunately, train service on Costa Rica's two main rail lines has been discontinued. The famous "Jungle Train" that ran from San José to the Caribbean port of Limón met its demise because of earthquake-caused landslides. Despite being a slow mode of transportation and more suited for tourists, this train ride was known for its breathtaking scenery. With any luck this railroad will open again.

Train service was also halted between San José and the Pacific port of Puntarenas. At present there is some talk of resuming this service in the future.

As if things weren't bad enough for those who enjoy train travel, train service has been further cut.

The Intertrain commuter service, unveiled with much fanfare two years ago between the western suburb of Pavas, San José and Cartago, now runs only between the University of Costa Rica in San Pedro and Heredia, with two runs in each direction Monday thorough Friday. The first run leaves San José for Heredia at 5:45 a.m. and returns at 6:30a.m. The afternoon run leaves the University of Costa Rica at 5:15 p.m., stops briefly in San José and continues to Heredia. The return trip leaves Heredia at 6:10 p.m. and goes as far San José. On Sundays, one run leaves San José at 10 a.m. and returns at 11a.m.

* NOTE: At any time train service throughout the country is subject to resumption or suspension.

OLD LIMON JUNGLE TRAIN

TAXIS AND AUTOMOBILE RENTALS

As we mentioned in Chapter 2, it is not necessary to own an automobile if you live in or near San José because taxis are plentiful and inexpensive. San José's buses are cheaper but taxis are the best way to get from point A to point B.

Taxis charge 100 colones for the first kilometer and 45 colones per kilometer thereafter. You can rent cabs by the hour for 600 to 1000 colones. There is also a charge for stopping time equivalent to the charge for one kilometer on the meter.

If you take a taxi between 10 p.m. and 5 a.m., the driver can charge 20 percent more than the meter fare. If you want the driver to wait while you do an errand or some other business, there is an hourly rate. If you have to go more than 12 kilometers outside the metropolitan area, there is another rate.

Nearly all taxis have computerized meters called **Marías**. Always insist that your taxi driver use his meter, and be sure to ask about rates before traveling anywhere.

If you are overcharged or dissatisfied with service, you can take the driver's permit number usually on the visor of his cab or his license number and complain to the MOPT Office (**Ministerio de Obras Públicas y Transporte**) at Plaza Víquez. You can do this in person, by letter or over the telephone.

Most taxi drivers know how to find those out of the way places and how to locate those almost non-existent addresses around San José. The majority of homes don't have numbers or addresses.

Around 2,500 taxis work in the San José area, so you should have no problem getting a taxi. They can be found around every public square and park, outside discotheques, on most busy streets and in front of government buildings and most hotels. Be careful since many taxis parked in front of hotels overcharge.

It is difficult to find a cab during the rainy season, especially in the afternoon when it usually rains. You may also have trouble getting a cab weekdays during rush hour between 7 a.m. and 9 a.m. and 4:30 p.m. to 6:30 p.m.—as in most cities. To hail a cab just yell, "Taxi!" If a cab is parked just say *"libre"* (free) to the driver to see if a cab is available. If the cab is available, he will usually nod or say, "sí" (yes).

If you want to stay on a cab drivers good side, NEVER slam the taxis doors; cabs are expensive in Costa Rica and drivers try to keep them in good shape.

Some people moonlight as taxi drivers using their own unmarked cars. They are called *piratas* (pirates) by the locals, and will often approach if they see you looking for a cab. Since they don't have meters, we advise you not to hire any of these vehicles for transportation.

If you call a cab, be able to give your exact location in Spanish, so the taxi driver knows where to pick you up. If you phone for a cab, the driver can turn on the meter when he gets the call and charge for the driving time to your location.

Airport pick-ups can be arranged in advance by calling one of the cab companies. We recommend doing this, especially during the rainy season, when it is difficult to get a cab when you need one.

Telephone numbers of the local cab companies are in the yellow pages of the telephone book under the heading "Taxi." The *Copeguari* taxi company(226-1366) has the most cabs available 24-hours a day(see the directory in the back of this book for a list of taxi companies).

Many of these companies also rent big trucks, or *Taxis de Carga*, at a very low hourly rate. These vehicles can be very helpful if you ever have to move furniture.

Major international car rental agencies and private car rentals are conveniently located all over San José. Most rental agencies operate like those in the United States. The cost of renting a vehicle depends on the year, model and make of car. You must be at least 18 years old and have a valid driver's license, an American Express, Visa or Master Card or be able to leave a large deposit. Remember, insurance is extra.

Always phone or make arrangements for car rentals well in advance. For a list of car rental agencies, see the phone directory we have provided in the back of this book, the yellow pages or the *Tico Times* for ads.

Also, in the *Tico Times* are ads for private drivers or chauffers. This is a good alternative to taxis but can be expensive. We know quite a few people who don't like to drive and prefer to hire private drivers instead of taking cabs whenever they have to do errands or other business.

DRIVING IN COSTA RICA

You may use your current driver's license for up to 90 days if you are a tourist. After 90 days must get a Costa Rican driver's license. At present foreigners cannot obtain a license unless they are Costa Rican residents. All permanent residents and *pensionados* must have a Costa Rican license to drive in Costa Rica.

It is relatively easy to obtain a license if you meet the requirements. First, go to the *Oficina de Transporte* where driver's licenses are issued. It's located one block west of Plaza Víquez on the southwest corner (Ave. 18 and Calle 5, Tel: 227-2188).

If you have a license from your own country, it's only a matter of transferring information, paying a small procesing fee (about $5–$7) taking an eye exam, having a little—or a lot of— patience and you will have your license in a matter of hours. It is valid for three years. If you don't have a current license or if your license has expired you have to take a driver's test and written exam as in the U.S. All this worthwhile if you plan to live and drive in Costa Rica.

One thing we would like to point out is that in most cases a driver's license is not a valid form of identification as in the U.S. In order to cash checks or identy yourself you need a passport or a *cédula*. The latter is issued only when you have permanent residency in Costa Rica.

Whether you are renting a car or using your own automobile, always keep the proper documents in your car. Check with your lawyer to see what documents are required. If you are a *pensionado* and your car has special *pensionado* plates, the police will occasionally stop you to see if your paperwork is in order. If a policeman should stop you, above all be polite, stay calm, and do not be verbally abusive. Most traffic police are courteous and helpful. However, if you commit a traffic violation, some policemen will try to have you pay for your ticket on the spot. Be advised this is not the standard procedure. If this happens to you, there are two offices where you can complain.

You can file your complaints with the Judicial Police (O.I.J.) or with the Legal Department of the Transit Police (227-2188). Finally, if you are involved in a traffic accident, **don't move your car** and be sure to contact the local traffic police (222-7150, 227-8030) so they can make out a report.

Be very careful when driving in San José or any other city. Most streets in San José are narrow, one-way and very crowded due to heavy traffic. Names of streets are not on sign posts on the street corners as in the United States. Most streets' names are on small blue signs on the sides of buildings. Some streets don't even have signs.

When driving in the countryside, drive only during the day, watch out for livestock, and be sure to use some kind of map. Don't get off the main paved road unless absolutely necessary during the rainy season if your car does not have four-wheel drive. You may end up getting stuck in the mud. Unfortunately, the only way to some of Costa Rica's best beaches and mountain resorts is by unpaved roads. So be careful!

While on this subject, let's say a word about potholes. The Costa Rican government tries to keep its paved roads in good shape, but can't keep up with the workload. So watch out for potholes and ruts in the pavement. Your car's shocks and suspension system will be grateful.

For your information there is a new book, "The Essential Road Guide for Costa Rica" by Bill Baker, designed to make driving easier. This book can be purchased from Bill Baker, Apartado 1185-1011, San José, Costa Rica or Fax: 220-14-15. If you live in the U.S. or Canada, write to 104 Halfmoon Circle H-3, Hypoluxo, Florida 33462 or call 1-800-881-8607. Costa Rica Books also sells this book. For more details please see the books we list in the back.

If you own your own car or plan to buy one, you will need automobile insurance. Please see the last section in Chapter 2.

KEEPING YOUR BEARINGS STRAIGHT

You can get confused in Costa Rica especially in San José, trying to find your way around. Except for the center of San José, streets have no names or numbers or they are not in a visible place. People use known landmarks to get around, to locate addresses, and give directions. If you are unfamiliar with this system it is almost impossible to find your way around, and easy to get lost. Don't worry, after you have lived in Costa Rica a while, you will get used to this system. In the event you get lost, you can always ask Costa Ricans for directions—provided you understand a little Spanish or they speak some English.

As you know, Costa Ricans are generally very friendly and are usually happy to help you find the address you are looking for. However, it is always a good idea to ask a second person, because most Ticos are embarassed to admit they don't know an address and will sometimes give you directions whether they know where you want to go or not.

Here are some basic tips on how to get around Costa Rica and understand how the street numbering works. It is somewhat easier to find your way in downtown San José because of the layout of the city. Avenues, or *Avenidas*, run east to west. All the odd numbered avenues are north of Central Avenue (*Avenida Central*). The even numbered avenues are south. Streets, or *Calles*, run north to south, with odd numbered streets east of Calle Central, and even numbered streets to the west.

If you get lost, looking for a street sign on the side of a building and counting by two's will usually help you get your bearings. Keep in mind that the word avenue is often abbreviated as *A* and streets as *C* when you get written directions.

To find your way around Costa Rica, you also need to know that 100 meters (*cien metros*) is another way of saying one block. Likewise, 50 meters (*cincuenta metros*) is a half-block and 150 meters (*ciento cincuenta metros*) a block and a half. The word *varas* (an old Spanish unit of measuremen almost a yard) is slang and often used instead of the word *metros*-meters, when giving directions.

Landmarks such as corner grocery stores (*pulperías*), churches, schools and other buildings are usually used with this metric block system to locate addresses. For example, in finding a house someone might say, "From Saint Paul's Church, 200 meters west and 300 south." In interpreting written directions you should also know that "M" stands for meters.

An old trick Costa Ricans often use for finding the four compass points may make it easier for you to get your bearings straight. The front doors of all churches in Costa Rica face west. So, if there is a church nearby, imagine yourself with your back to the entrance of the church—you're facing west.

If you live in San José, there is another method for finding the compass points. Volcano Poás is north, the Cruz de Alajuela mountain, approximately south, the direction of Cartago is east and the general direction of the Sabana or Rohrmoser is west. This system of using landmarks should make it easier for you to find your way around the city.

DOWNTOWN SAN JOSE

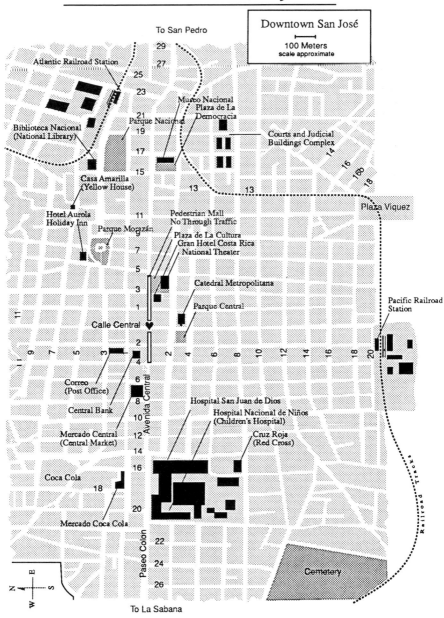

To San Pedro

Downtown San José

|—————|
100 Meters
scale approximate

Atlantic Railroad Station

29
27
25
23
21
19
17
15
13
11
9
7
5
3
1

Museo Nacional
Plaza de La
Democracia

Parque Nacional

Biblioteca Nacional
(National Library)

Courts and Judicial
Buildings Complex

Casa Amarilla
(Yellow House)

Plaza Viquez

Hotel Aurola
Holiday Inn

Parque Morazán

Pedestrian Mall
No Through Traffic

Plaza de La Cultura
Gran Hotel Costa Rica
National Theater

Catedral Metropolitana

Pacific Railroad
Station

Parque Central

Calle Central

Correo
(Post Office)

Central Bank

Avenida Central

Hospital San Juan de Dios

Hospital Nacional de Niños
(Children's Hospital)

Mercado Central
(Central Market)

Cruz Roja
(Red Cross)

Coca Cola

Mercado Coca Cola

Paseo Colón

Railroad Tracks

Cemetery

To La Sabana

N E S W

* **Courtesy of Bill Baker**

CHAPTER SIX

Communications

6.

TELEPHONE SERVICES

Costa Rica has the greatest number of telephones per capita of any Latin American country and boasts one of the world's best telephone systems, with direct dialing to more than 60 countries. Calls within the country are a bargain; you can call any place in the country for only a few cents. If your house or apartment doesn't have a phone, don't worry. Public telephones are just about everywhere in Costa Rica and use 5, 10, and 20 colón coins. If you don't have your own phone and want to make a direct international call, go to **Radiográfica,** telephone office, (open 7 a.m. to 10 p.m.) in downtown San José at Calle 1, Ave. 7, across from LACSA. You can place a collect long distance call from any phone booth by dialing 114. You can also make long distance calls from most hotels. From private phones in homes or offices, the procedure is just like in the U. S. by direct dialing or first talking to the operator *(operadora)*. The access numbers for calling Costa Rica from abroad are 011-506 plus the rest of the number.

In April of 1994, all phone numbers in Costa Rica were changed from six to seven digits. Most phone numbers now have an additional digit before the first number. In some cases the third number was changed. A two was inserted before most numbers in San José. The last four digits of each number remained the same. We are using the new phone numbers in this edition. This new system is bound to cause confusion at first, so if you have problems, look in the telephone book or dial 113 for assistance; the operator will help you.

Purchasing a telephone can be a real "pain in the neck" depending on where you live and the number of available lines. You can expect to wait from one to three months for phone installation after paying around $300 for this service. To have a phone installed, go to the I.C.E. office on the north side of Sabana Park, or call 220-7720. You can pay phone bills at the I.C.E. office there or at their office in downtown San José (Ave. 2, Calle 1) or any other I.C.E. ofice in Costa Rica. You can also pay at any of the Mas X Menos or Periféricos supermarkets.

Cellular phone service is available in Costa Rica. Call 257-2527 to get hooked up to the local cellular network.

Sending a FAX is very easy in Costa Rica. You can go *Radiográfica* (Tel: 287-0513, 287-0511) or *Telecomunicaciones Internacionales* (Tel: 257-2272). At the Radiográfica office you can send a fax or have them sent to you. You can also call their office to see they have received a fax for you. They will even call when a fax comes in if they have your phone number. Many private businesses offer fax services to individuals. You can usually find their number in the classified section of the *Tico Times* or *Costa Rica Today*.

Computer buffs will be pleased to know they may subscribe to almost any of the world's computer networks like CompuServe. Just go to the *Radiográfica* offices and open a RACSAPAC account to get connected to information highway. For further information about these services call 287-0358.

IMPORTANT TELEPHONE NUMBERS

BILINGUAL TOURIST INFORMATION... 257-4667 Ext: 1008
POLICE 117
PARAMEDICS 118
FIRE DEPARTMENT 118
ELECTRIC COMPANY 126
RURAL GUARD 127
AMBULANCE... 128
BILINGUAL EMERGENCY SERVICE (Like our 911) 122
RED CROSS AMBULANCE 221-5815
PUBLIC MEDICAL CENTERS
    HOSPITAL MEXICO 232-6122

MAIL

Costa Rica's postal system or *Cortel* (Correos *y Telégrafos de Costa Rica)* offers postal services comparable to that in many countries abroad.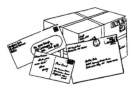

Just as in the United States, mail is received and sent from the post office *(correo or casa de correos.)* The main post office is in the heart of downtown San José at Calle 2, Ave. 1-3 (223-9766). Others mall cities and towns in rural areas have their own centrally located post offices. Airmail between the United States or Europe and Costa Rica usually takes about five to ten days. At present, an airmail letter to the U.S. or Canada costs 30 cents or 55 colones. An airmail stamp to Europe is about five cents more. *Cortel* also provides other services, including M-bags for sending large quantities of books or other printed matter abroad, telegrams, fax service, courier services and delivery of documents.

Please keep in mind that mail boxes are few and far between as are house numbers, so we recommend using your nearest post office for all postal related matters. Obtain a post office box *(apartado)* from your local post office in Costa Rica to ensure prompt and efficient mail service. To apply for a post office box, go to the post office nearest your office or home to fill out an application *(solicitud de apartado)*. The yearly rental fee ranges between ten and thirty or forty dollars depending on the size of the post office box. These P.O. boxes are in great demand, but you can usually get one in January, when most people give up leases on their boxes.

You may also receive mail in the general delivery section *(lista de correos)* of your local post office. This is especially useful in isolated regions of the country. Register at the nearest post office and they will put your name on the local *lista de correos*. When you pick up your mail, you pay a few cents per letter for this service. All letters must have your name, the phrase *lista de correos* and the name of the nearest post office.

Do you plan on having money from abroad sent to you in Costa Rica? The fastest and safest way to receive money while visiting or residing in Costa Rica is to have an international money order shipped to you by one of the worldwide courier services, such as DHL or UPS. Letters and small packages usually take about two working days (Mon.–Fri.) to reach Costa Rica from the United States or Canada.

U. S. banks can wire money to banks in Costa Rica. This method is safe, but slow, as many bureaucratic delays can develop while waiting for checks to clear. The Costa Rican postal service is planning to start a money order service allowing money orders to be sent from the U.S. to Costa Rica. This service promises to be much faster and much more economical than getting money wired to your bank in Costa Rica.

Western Union in Costa Rica boasts that they offer the fastest money transfers in the country. They claim that their network of Western Union agencies around the world can send money or a message to anyone anywhere quickly, securely and more easily than their competitors. Call Western Union at 257-1312 or 257-1150 for additional information or go to one of the following agencies.

In or near San José:

LOS YOSES - Cambios y Servicios de San José, 20 meters south of the Fátima Church.

TIBAS - Centro Comercial Ana, Carolina #7, 250 meters west of

the Palacio Municipal (city hall)
LA SOLEDAD - Contiguo a Tica Bus, Calle 9, Ave. 2 y 4, San José.
ESCAZU - Multiservicios Secretariales, 25 meters east of post office.

In other parts of the country:
LIBERIA - Cambios y Servicios de San José, Agroagencia buildings across from National Bank.
SAN ISIDRO GENERAL - Centro Comercial (shopping center) Placita Pere next to the bank of Costa Rica
PUNTARENAS - Veleros del Sur, S.A. across from the I.C.E. Substation in El Cocal.

Many money changers *(cambistas)* have private offices near the central post office and banks in downtown San José. Some of these money changers will cash personal checks from your U. S. checking account when they know you. You can get the name of a money changer from other retirees or residents.

You can have Social Security and Veteran's benefits mailed to you directly through the U.S. Embassy, once you have established a permanent residence in Costa Rica. However, these checks usually don't arrive until sometime after the tenth of each month.

The worst way to send money is through the regular mail. People report that many checks have been lost or stolen. Postal thieves are very sophisticated in Costa Rica and work with black market money changers. The postal system has received numerous complaints and has promised to do something about them.

If you need to file a complaint about lost or stolen mail, go to *Cortel's* complaint department *(Departamento de Reclamaciones)* in downtown San José on Ave. 6, between Calles 17 and 19. If you live outside San José, you can file a complaint at any local post office and it will be forwarded to San José.

If you still choose to use the regular mail system after reading the above, be sure to have your checks or money orders sent to you in security, non-transparent manila envelope—ones that can't be seen through when held up to a light.

The rash of postal thefts, prompts more and more people to use the new private-mail companies that offer a variety of postal related services.
Aerocasillas (P.O. Box 4567–1000, San José, Costa Rica, Tel: 255-4567; Fax 257-1187); **Trans-Express "Interlink"** (Tel: 232-2544); **AAA Express Mail** (Tel: 233-9993; Fax: 221-5056); and **Star Box** (P.O. Box

405–1000, San José, Tel: 221-9029, 221-4744; Fax: 233-0448) are a few of the better mail companies which provide clients with a mail drop and P.O. Box in Miami, and a physical address where they can send or receive mail. This enables customers living in Costa Rica to have their mail sent to the Miami address where the companies forward the mail to Costa Rica.

These companies provide much faster service than the Costa Rican mail system to access to mail order products from the U.S., to enable clients to subscribe to magazines and newspapers at U.S. domestic rates, and to help obtain replacement parts from abroad. You can even have your packages picked up and delivered to your home or office at any time you decide.

Rates run from about 15 to 45 dollars per month depending on the amount of mail you receive and whether you have a business or personal account.

The worst time to receive any correspondence through the regular Costa Rican mail is between November 20 and January 1st. Letters can be delayed up to a month by the enormous volume of Christmas mail and the vacations of postal workers during the month of December.

You should avoid having anything larger than a letter or a magazine sent to you in Costa Rica. Any item bigger than that will be sent to the customs warehouse (aduana) and you will make several trips to get it out.

On the first trip to customs your package or parcel is unwrapped so you can fill out a declaration of its contents. On the second trip you usually will have to pay an exorbitant duty, equivalent to the value of the item plus the mailing cost. If you refuse to pay, your package will be confiscated—not sent back—just confiscated.

So as you can see, because of the costs involved and wasted time, it is better to have friends bring you large items, pick them up when you're visiting the states, or use one of the private mail companies mentioned in this section.

CHAPTER SEVEN

Lodging and Cuisine

7.

LODGING

While exploring Costa Rica or looking for an apartment, house or some other residence, you may choose to stay at one of the many accommodations listed below.

We have even included aparthotels, a cross between an apartment and a hotel, as the name implies. If you are living in Costa Rica only on a seasonal basis, one of these aparthotels is probably your best bet. Most have a kitchenette or other cooking facilities. Usually they are less expensive than hotels with similar amenities, but more expensive than apartments. One of the best is the **Lamm**. Many of our friends have stayed there and like its convenient downtown location. Its spacious apartments are a real plus. **The Don Carlos** and **Los Yoses** are also centrally located and have nice accomodations.

Bread-and-Breakfasts, or B & B's as they are sometimes called,have sprouted-up all over Costa Rica in recent years. Most of these establishments are smaller and in many cases, less expensive than hotels. What sets them apart from other lodging is their home-like, quaint ambience. Many have a live-in host or owner on the premises and some are downtown. Most B & B's advertise in the local English newspapers, but there is now a service to help you find the "right" B&B for you. Call or fax the Bread-and-Breakfast Association at 228-9200.

We have tried to list a wide variety of accommodations to select from. Taking all personal budgets into consideration, we have divided them into the following categories according to their approximate rates; Expensive— $85 and above; Moderately priced— $35 to $85; Low priced— below $35; and the Lowest priced— below $20.

EXCELLENT HOTELS
(Downtown or near downtown San José.)
AMBASSADOR - Moderately priced 221-8155
BALMORAL - Moderately priced 222-5022
CAMINO REAL - Very expensive, too far from town ... 289-7000
CARIARI HOTEL - Expensive, has a golf course 239-0022
COROBICI - Expensive 232-8122
HOTEL DEL REY-All prices, a favorite with *gringos* 221-7272
EUROPA - Moderately priced... 222-1212
GRAN HOTEL COSTA RICA - Moderately priced 221-4000
GRAND DE ORO - Expensive (Quaint) 255-3322
EJECUTIVO NAPOLEON - Expensive 223-32-52
HOTEL AUROLA HOLIDAY INN - Expensive 233-7233
HOTEL PRESIDENTE - Moderately priced 222-2034
IRAZU - Moderately priced 232-4811
SAN JOSE PALACIO - Expensive 220-2034

NICE HOTELS
(Downtown or near downtown San José.)
AMSTEL - Moderately priced 222-4622
BOUGAINVILLEA - Moderately priced 233-6622
DON CARLOS - Moderately priced 221-6707
DUNN INN - A renowned *gringo* hangout 222-3232
LA GRAN VIA - Moderately priced 222-7737
ROYAL DUTCH - Moderately priced 222-1414
SAN JOSE GARDEN COURT - Moderately priced 255-4766
TENNIS CLUB - Moderately priced 232-1266

APARTHOTELS
(Downtown or near downtown San José.
Some with kitchens, telephones and televisions available)
APARTAMENTOS SCOTLAND - Weekly or monthly . 223-0833
CASTILLA - Moderately low priced 222-2113
D'GALAH - Moderately low priced .... 234-1743 or 253-7539
EL CONQUISTADOR - Moderately low priced 225-3022
APARTHOTEL LA SABANA - Moderately priced 220-2422

LAMM - Moderately low priced 221-4920
NAPOLEON - Moderately low priced 223-3252
RAMGO - Moderately low priced. 232-3823

MORE AFFORDABLE PLACES TO STAY
(Downtown or near downtown San José.
Clean safe rooms - some with meals.)

CASA MARIA DE ESCAZU - Low priced 228-2270
COSTA RICA INN - Low priced 222-5203
DIPLOMAT - Low priced 221-8133
GALILEA - Low priced 233-6925
HOTEL ALAMEDA - Low priced 221-3045
HOTEL CACTS - Budget hotel 221-8616
HOTEL PARK - *Gringo* hangout 221-6944
HOTEL TALAMANCA - Low priced 233-5033
PETIT HOTEL - Reasonably priced 233-0766
PICO BLANCO - Low priced, great view 228-3197
PLAZA - Low priced 222-5533
RITZ - Low priced 222-4103

INEXPENSIVE PLACES TO STAY
(Downtown or near downtown San José.
* Private baths; ** Some shared)

* ** ASTORIA - The lowest priced 221-2172
    BELLAVISTA - The lowest priced 223-0095
*   CORCORI - The lowest priced 233-0081
*   GRAN HOTEL CENTRAL AMERICA - Good for
    the handicapped 221-3362
*   HOTEL JOHNSON - Low priced 223-7633
* ** MARLIN - The lowest priced 233-3212
    MUSOC - Low priced, next to bus station 222-9497
** TORUMA YOUTH HOSTEL - Inexpensive 222-4085
** TROY'S HOTEL - One block east of museum 222-6756

BED & BREAKFAST
(Small, quaint, and generally, but not necessarily inexpensive,
downtown or near downtown San José)

PENSION DE LA CUESTA 255-2896
POSADA PEGASUS: Escazú 228-4196
LINDA VISTA LODGE: Escazú 228-5199

GRAN HOTEL COSTA RICA

RESTAURANTS

Many excellent restaurants serving a wide variety of international foods are scattered all over the San José area. Most of these restaurants are incredible bargains when compared to similar establishments in the United States. You will be happy to know that Costa Rica's restaurants are clean and health codes are strictly enforced by the Health Department *(Ministerio de Salud)*. For your convenience we have included a list of our favorite places to eat but you are sure to discover many on your own or by word of mouth once you have lived in Costa Rica for a while.

La Princesa Marina (232-0481) offers some of the best sea food you will ever savor. Try their foot-long trout or shrimp cocktails. Chinese restaurants abound in San José and all over Costa Rica. There are also many Italian restaurants. **Valerios** (225-0838) has great pizza and pasta. If you like U.S.-style food and beer served in foot-tall mugs, try **Fridays** near the university in San Pedro. As we mention in Chapter 9, **La Soda Tapia** is famous for its gigantic fruit salads and typical breakfasts.

Lovers of Mexican food should try any of the **Antojitos** restaurants. **La Cascada** in Los Anonos has very tasty fish and meat dishes. The **Soda Palace,** across from the Central Park is open 24-hours and is a good place to grab a late night snack.

The **Pops** ice cream parlors sell every imaginable flavor of your favorite ice cream.

Coffee connoisseurs can savor a cup of their favorte local brew and grab a bite to eat at the **Café Parisien** in the Gran Hotel Costa Rica, **La Esquina del Café** or **La Casa Verde** in Barrio Amón and **Café Mundo** downtown.

If you like to eat-on-the-run, you can, because all of the American fast food restaurant chains are operating in Costa Rica.

If you are on a tight budget, try eating at San José's *Central Market* (Calle 6 and Avenida Central). You'll find 10 to 15 small restaurants, called *sodas*, where a complete meal costs between one and three dollars.

Here are some of San José's most popular dining establishments. Prices vary but in general most are reasonable. The *Tico Times* and

Costa Rica Today both carry advertisements for restaurants and weekly restaurant reviews

AMSTEL HOTEL (different cuisines) 233-6622
BALCON DE EUROPA (Italian cuisine) 221-4841
CHALET SUIZO (different cuisines) 222-3118
FLOR DE LOTO (Hunan & Szechuan Chinese) 232-4652
GOYA (Spanish food)
HOTEL BOUGAINVILLA RESTAURANT (good food)...... 233-6622
LA FUENTE DE MARISCOS (seafood) 231-0631
L'ILE (French) 222-4241
LA MASIA DE TRIQUELL (Spanish) 221-5073
LA NUEVA CHINA (Chinese) 224-4478
PAPRIKA (rich tasting food) 225-8971
PICCOLA ROMA (Italian) 223-1073
RESTAURANT VILLA BONITA (best Chinese food
   in San José) 232-9855
STEAK HOUSE LOS RANCHOS (meat dishes
   Sabana Norte) 232-7757
VIA VENETO (Italian) 234-2898

MORE AFFORDABLE DINING

CHARLEY'S BAR AND GRILL — Cajun and North American food
CHIPS — International food in Plaza de la Cultura
CONFETTI'S — Nice opposite the Plaza de La Democracia
GRAND DE ORO — In a hotel
HOTEL PICO BLANCO— Great view of San José and very romantic
LA SODA TAPIA — Best breakfasts in San José
LAS TUNAS — Barbequed beef, seafood, Mexican food and disco
LA HACIENDA DE LOS PANCHOS — Authentic Mexican Food
LA HACIENDA STEAK HOUSE — Downtown
LOUISIANA — Cajun-style food on the road to Escazú
MACCHU PICHU — Peruvian dishes
MANOLO'S — Good food
MIRO'S BISTRO — Italian and American
PANADERIA SCHMIDT — Fantastic pastries, Avenida Central
PIZZA METRO — Unique pizza, downtown
PIPO'S — Great sandwiches
POLLO CAMPESINO — Delicious chicken
RISAS — Bar and restaurant with American-style food
ROSTI POLLO — Great chicken cooked over coffee wood

SPOON —Best of desserts (three locations)
TEQUILA WILLY'S —Good Tex-Mex food, fun
TIQUICIA — Costa Rican food and a fantastic wiew of San José
TORINO — Caribbean style food in Tibás

VEGETARIAN EATERIES
DITSO — One of San José's newest whole foods restaurants
DON SOL — Complete cuisine
LA MACROBIOTICA — Good food
LA MAZORCA — Great macrobiotic lunches
NUTRISODA — Next to Gran Hotel Costa Rica
SHAKTI — Vegetarian goodies
VISHNU — Several locations, inexpensive

FAST FOOD & TAKE OUT
PIZZA HUT (Home delivery available)
    Plaza del Sol 253-3636
    La California.. 255-2828
    Rohrmoser 220-1818
    Escazú 228-9898
DOMINO PIZZA (Home delivery)
    San Pedro 225-3030
    Centro Comercial Los Anonos 228-9595
KENTUCKY FRIED CHICKEN
    Paseo Colón 222-3795
    Ave Ctl, C 31, Los Yoses 225-9812
    Avenida Segunda 221-8397
BURGER KING
    San Perdo
    Sabana Norte (North)
    Parque Central
McDONALD'S
    Plaza de La Cultura
    Plaza del Sol
    Sabana Sur
    Ave. Ctl., Calle 4 (downtown)
TACO BELL
    San Pedro (opposite the university)
    La Plaza de La Cultura

CHAPTER EIGHT

Red Tape

DEALING WITH BUREAUCRACY

Just as in the rest of Latin America, Costa Rica is plagued by a more inefficient bureaucratic systemthan is U. S. This situation is exaggerated by the Latin American temperament, seemingly lackadaisical attitude of most bureaucrats and the slower pace of life south of the border. The concept of time is much different from that in the U. S. or Canada. When someone says they'll do something *"ahorita'* (which literally means right now), it will take from a few minutes to a week, or maybe forever. It is not unusual to wait in lines for hours in banks and government offices and experience unnecessary delays that would seldom occur the U. S.

This situation is very frustrating for foreigners, who are used to fast, efficient service. It can be especially irritating if you don't speak good Spanish. Since very few people working in offices speak English and most North Americans speak little else, it is advisable to study basic Spanish. However, if language is an insurmountable obstacle at first, use a competent bilingual lawyer or ask the *Costa Rican Residents Association* to help you deal with Costa Rica's bureaucracy or "red tape jungle" as it is known. Above all, learn to be patient and remember that you can get the best results if you do not push or pressure people. Try having a good sense of humor and using a smile. You will be surprised at the results.

You shouldn't despair if Costa Rica's "bureaucrazy" gets you down. For a small fee you can get a person (*tramitador)* to wait in line for you while you run errand or make better use of your valuable time.

A few words of caution—there are some individuals, (*chorizeros* in popular jargon), who pass themselves off as lawyers or who befriend you and offer to help you with red tape, claiming they can short-cut the bureaucratic system because of their contacts. As a general rule, avoid such individuals or you will lose valuable time, run the risk of acquiring forged documents, most certainly lose money and experience indescribable grief. Since bribery is an institution in most Latin American countries and government employees are underpaid, some people advise paying them extra money to speed up paper work or circumvent normal channels. This bribery is illegal and not recommended for foreigners; they can be deported for breaking the law. However, in some instances it may be necessary to pay extra money to get things done. Use your own discretion in such matters.

Everyone planning to live or retire in Costa Rica should know that the American Embassy, (in the San José suburb of Pavas), can help with: Social Security and Veterans benefits, notarizing documents, obtaining new U. S. passports, registering births of your children and getting a U.S. visa for your spouse (if you chose to marry a Costa Rican). They also assist in obtaining absentee ballots for U.S. elections and getting U.S. income tax forms and information. If you get into any legal trouble in Costa Rica, do not expect help from the U.S. Embassy.

HOW TO BECOME A LEGAL RESIDENT OF COSTA RICA

You can live in Costa Rica for six months a year by getting extensions on your visa. Tourists may remain legally in the country for six months without having to apply for permanent residency. You may own property, start a business or make investments with no more than a tourist visa.

We know many Americans, Canadians and other foreigners who started businesses as tourists. If you plan to reside in Costa Rica full-time, however, one of Costa Rica's permanent residency programs will appeal to you.

Several residency categories permit you to retain your current citizenship and obtain long-term legal status in Costa Rica. They are *resident pensionado, pensionado rentista,* and *rentista inversionista* (resident investor). Which program you choose depends on your needs and financial position.

In March of 1992 a change in the pensionado law eliminated many tax privileges retirees had enjoyed since the program started in 1964.

Under the old system foreigners with official *pensionado* or *rentista* (permanent retiree) status, were required to live in the country four months a year. They were entitled to the following perks: permanent residency without immigration hassles; all the privileges of Costa Rican citizens, except the right to vote and work for hire; the right to import duty-free one of each of the major appliances such as refrigerator, stove, microwave, television, washer and dryer, and many unlimited personal household goods.

Pensionados could import a new car every five years duty-free, provided it was worth less than $16,000.00. In 1992, low taxes on imported cars and duty-free household goods were eliminated. Since then, all *pensionados* have to pay taxes on their automobiles and household goods the same as ordinary Costa Rican citizens do.

The rest of the *pensionado's* privileges remain pretty much intact, the most notable of which is permanent residency so you can stay in the country legally. So, we suggest you consider these facts before deciding if it is advantageous for you to become a *pensionado*.

Despite this new law, Costa Rica is still an attractive retirement haven since the country offers so much. People flock to Costa Rica because of its peaceful atmosphere, excellent climate, friendly people and natural beauty instead of tax exonerations on a few luxury items. The Costa Rican government has reduced taxes on some cars and other imported goods, making them affordable for most Costa Ricans as well as foreign residents. This eliminates the need for the tax-exoneration program.

If it is absolutely necessary to have an automobile, you can bring a car from the states if it is five years old or older and pay only a few thousand dollars tax on it. You can also go to Golfito the free port in southern Costa Rica, and buy a stove, refrigerator or other appliance without paying high import duties.

A lawsuit has been filed on behalf of the *pensionados*, by the *Pensionado* Association, (now called the **Costa Rican Residents Association),** in response to the elimination of their tax privileges. Rumors circulate that many of the pensionado's perks will be restored in the future. So, there is now a glimmer of hope that this law will be changed. On a more encouraging note, in mid-1993, all persons who were *pensionados* prior to April 1992, regained some of their rights and privileges as a result of a court decision.

Now let's look at the requirements and specific documents that you will need to present to the Costa Rican government if you choose to apply for the *resident pensionado, pensionado rentista* categories.

A **Resident Pensionado** is someone who lives on a pension (a U.S. Social Security check or permanent retirement program). A husband and wife cannot combine their pensions but the wife can live under the husband's *pensionado* status or visa versa. If the recipient of the pension dies, the spouse can retain *pensionado* status if the pension is inherited. Some paper work, naturally, is involved.

Here are the requirements for this category:

Resident Pensionado
1. A lifetime income of at least $600 a month generated outside of Costa Rica.
2. A signed letter confirming that you will receive this money in Costa Rica.
3. A letter from a C.P.A. stating that you will receive the $600 for life, if the pension comes from a company's pension plan.
4. If the money comes from a company, two letters from bank officials showing that your company is financially sound and that the pension plan has been in existence for at least 20 years.
5. A detailed account of your company's pension plan.

As a *pensionado* you are obligated to exchange $7,200 ($600 per month) a year for colones at a government bank. You need proof of this to update your file. If you can't prove that you converted enough money during the year, you can lose your status. You also have to renew your *pensionado* I.D. card every two years and reside in the country for at least four months yearly. As a *pensionado* you can own and operate your own business.

Pensionado Rentista is a residency category designed for those who are not retired and receive no government pension. To qualify for *rentista* status, you must have an income of $12,000 a year ($1,000 per month) comming from an investment or annuity. A good way to do this is to buy a certificate of deposit at a Costa Rican bank that generates a monthly income of at least $1000.

As a *rentista* you must prove that this investment will be stable for at least five years. At the end of five years, you have to prove your source of income again. Furthermore, every year as a *rentista* you have to prove that you changed $12,000 into colones and show your passport to prove you were in the country at least four months.

As a *pensionado rentista* you can own and operate a business. The disadvantage to being a *rentista* is tying up your funds for five years.

In brief to qualify for *pensionado rentista* status you need:

1. An income of $1,000 per month for the next five years in Costa Rica.
2. Documentation that attests to the company or bank's solvency, if the income is from a foreign source.

Rentista Inversionista is another permanent resident status for people who are not retired and want to invest in Costa Rica. If you have a lot of money to invest, this might be the best route to go. The goverrnment will grant residency under this category if you invest at least $50,000 in high priority projects like tourism or reforestation or $200,000 in any other business.

The paperwork and requirements are similar to the other residency programs, but there are a few basic differences. Under this program you must reside in Costa Rica at least six months of every year and live as a temporary residency for two years. After the initial two year-period you are eligible to become a permanent resident.

If you plan to start a project, additional paperwork—such as a feasibility study and bank references—may be needed. If you are going to get involved in tourism, you will need permission from the Costa Rican Tourism Institute (I.T.C.). When investing in an established company, you will have to show the company's books.

Since every circumstance is different, contact the Residents Association for a good lawyer to answer your questons.

The following other documents are required for *pensionado, rentista, rentista-inversionista* (resident investor) and most other residency categories:

1. An application to the Director of Intelligence and Security.
2. Medical examinations performed by the corresponding departments of the Costa Rican Ministry of Public Health.
3. The formal application should have the following information: your mother's maiden name, full name, nationality, passport number, dependent's names, date of entry into Costa Rica, origin and amount of income, address in country of origin or Costa Rica; authentication by a notary public and corresponding stamps.
4. A sworn notarized declaration stating that you won't work in

Costa Rica; that if you leave the country you will notify I.C.T.; that you will spend four months a year in Costa Rica; that you have no police record; that you will exchange the required number of dollars each month at a national bank.

5. Police Certificate from your local area stating that you have no record. (This document is good for only six months, so make sure it is current.)

6. Birth Certificate

7. Marriage certificate if applicable

8. Certified copy of your entire passport

9. Certificate of non-residence

10. Twelve passport size photos—6 front view and 6 profile

11. Don't forget that all of these required documents must be translated into Spanish by an official translator.

If you meet the prerequisites for any of the residency categories and have gathered all the required documents, you are ready to apply for your chosen status.

Next, have the Costa Rican Residents Association or an attorney present your papers to the tourist board (I.C.T.), who will process them in two months or so.

If you want to avoid the many inconveniences of Costa Rica's giant "bureaucrazy" and save time and money in the long run, join the **Costa Rican Residents Association.** This excellent organization formerly called the Pensionado Association, changed its name in July 1992 when the *pensionado* law changed.

The association has been reorganized and revitalized and now offers services to all legal residents in Costa Rica, not just the *pensionados.*

For a small membership fee of $50, the Costa Rican Residents Association, at Casa Canada two blocks south of Centro Colón on the corner of Avenida 4 and Calle 40, will assist you when you need help applying for *pensionado* or other residency status (for $1,000 which is a good deal since many lawyers charge up to $2,000 and take much longer). It can also help in buying and selling cars, getting a Costa Rican driver's license (see chapter 5 for details); assisting with English to Spanish translations of any required documents or papers and making sure your annual papers are up-to-date. The association can also notarize all your important documents; help with the renewal of your I.D. card or *cédula* and help you obtain medical coverage with the Costa Rican Social Security System and the new supplemental coverage they (The Residents Association) now offer (see the section on medical care for details). Should you desire additional information, contact:

Costa Rican Resident's Association
Apartado 700-1011
San José, Costa Rica
Call: 333-8068 or 221-2053 inside Costa Rica and 011-506-333-8068 outside the country. Fax 011 506-222-7862.
Address in the U.S. for your convenience:
Costa Rican Resident's Association
P.O. Box 025292-SB19
Miami, Florida 33102-5292
or contact:
Departamento de Rentistas
Instituto Costarricense de Turismo
(Costa Rican Tourism Institute)
Apartado, 777-1000
San José, Costa Rica
011-506-223-1733, Ext. 264

The Costa Rican Tourism Institute now has a toll-free number to call from abroad for answers to all your questions about Costa Rica. Call 1-800-343-6332 or Fax: 011-506-255-4997.

ADDITIONAL METHODS OF OBTAINING COSTA RICAN RESIDENCY

As we mentioned in the last section, most of the *pensionado* program's privileges were revoked in 1992, so the only real advantage for becoming a *pensionado* is to be able to stay in the country legally. Now more and more people are looking at other ways of obtaining Costa Rican residency.

Basically, the residency program is for people wanting to reside in Costa Rica full-time but who cannot qualify for *pensionado* or *rentista* status or for those who can qualify, but choose not to because some of the advantages were taken away.

There are several other ways for foreigners to obtain legal

residency. As we mentioned in the last section, they can become *residente inversionistas* (resident investors) by investing $50,000 in a priority project such as reforestation, tourism, exports or $200,000 in anything else.

Foreigners can also claim residency if they have an immediate relative in Costa Rica, a child, spouse or parent. They must also prove they have financial means to support themselves while living in Costa Rica (about $600 per month). Relatives of foreigners who have become Costa Rican residents are also eligible for residency.

Marrying a Costa Rican also entitles you to residency. This is the fastest way to become a resident. We know of many expatriates who have married Costa Ricans for this very reason.

In addition, anyone who has lived for at least two years under another residency category, such as *pensionado* or *rentista*, may apply for Costa Rican residency. Many ex-*pensionados* are doing this, because they can generally qualify for this status easily. With this type of residency you have to live in the country six months a year.

As in the case of the other residency catagories you need an application, birth certificate, maritial status certificate, police report, several passport photos and in some cases documents proving your relationship to your Costa Rican relatives.

Temporary residency, *residencia temporal*, is for students enrolled in a university or language school, Peace Corps volunteers and members of affiliated church service groups. Language teachers at any language institute in San José may obtain temporary residency enabling them to stay in the country legally. Others doing jobs that Costa Ricans cannot do are also eligible for this status.

Because each person's situation is different, the procedure is complicated. All residency programs require mounds of paper work, so we advise you to consult a lawyer to facilitate this process. To find a competent, trustworthy attorney, go to the Costa Rican Residents Association office after reading the section in this chapter titled, "How to Find a Lawyer."

There was an additional way to acquire residency. Foreigners who resided in Costa Rica after July 31, 1993 with no criminal record could apply for Costa Rican residency to get a *cédula* (residency card). This had to be done during an amnesty period that lasted until mid-April of 1994.

Most of the readers of this book would not have qualified for this special residency program, but we thought that it deserved mention in this section.

IMMIGRATION AND OTHER MATTERS

PERPETUAL TOURIST

If you don't want to invest the time and money to become a *pensionado* or resident, you can live as a perpetual tourist in Costa Rica. No paper work or lawyers need be involved. Just leave the country every three months to renew your tourist visa. All you have to do is leave the country for at least 72 hours. You can repeat this process over-and-over again to stay in Costa indefinitely. The only disadvantage is that as a tourist you can't work in Costa Rica and it is almost impossible to become a legal resident, unless you marry a Costa Rican or have immediate Costa Rican relatives.

If you don't want to bother leaving the country every few months to renew your papers, you can stay in the country illegally, and pay a small fine when you leave. The fine is about five dollars a month. We have personally met many people who have lived as tourists for years without problems; some even started businesses.

Bear in mind that it is always better to have your papers up-to-date because you can be deported almost instantly if you get into any kind of trouble and are in the country illegally.

EXTENDING YOUR STAY

Every tourist with a valid passport (U.S. citizens, Canadians and most Europeans) has permission to remain in Costa Rica without a visa for up to 90 days.

U.S. citizens and Canadian citizens may enter the country with just a 30-day tourist card and another piece if identification such as a driver's license, passport or birth certificate.

You can get tourist cards from any Costa Rican consulate or embassy prior to your trip or at the airline ticket counter on the day you leave for Costa Rica. Tourist cards can be renewed monthly by applying for an extension called a *prórroga de turismo*. To obtain this extention you will need your passport, a ticket out of the country (see the section titled Bus Travel to and From Costa Rica in Chapter 5), three passport-size photos, and at least $200 in cash or travelers' checks for each additional month you're staying.

This process takes a couple of days and is a bureaucratic nightmare. To save yourself many headaches, long lines and time, you should go to any local travel agency. Most of the agencies in San José will help extend your tourist card or obtain an exit visa for about $5, even if you didn't purchse your ticket there. This service is worthwhile and usually takes two working days. Remember if you overstay your tourist visa you will have to pay a fine when you leave the country.

The immigration offices are in the suburb of La Uruca, near the Irazú Hotel.

LEAVING THE COUNTRY

Any tourist who has stayed in Costa Rica more than 30 days with just a tourist card will need an exit visa or *visa de salida* to leave the country. Likewise, foreigners who entered Costa Rica using just a passport and overstayed the maximum permitted time of 90 days, will also have to get an exit visa.

To obtain this documant you first need *pensión alimenticia* stamps to prove you haven't left dependent children behind. Go to the court buildings or *Tribunales de Justicia* (Calle 17, Aves. 6-8) for these stamps. Then take your passport, the stamps and your return ticket to the Immigration Office to get an exit visa. The whole process takes two working days. As we just mentioned above, most tourist agencies will do all of the running around for a small fee.

One good thing about having to obtain an exit visa is that it is valid for 30 days from date it is issued. You can stay in the country another thirty days using this extention, so you can remain in Costa Rica for 120 days.

For a longer stay, wait until your 90 days have expired and apply for a two-month visa extension near the end of the fourth month. This way you can remain in the country for six-months at a time without any problems.

Costa Rican citizens, retirees and permanent residents must also get an exit visa and *pension alimenticia* stamps. A foreigner living under any of the three residency categories will pay about $40 for an exit visa.

CHILDREN'S EXIT VISAS

Children under 18, including infants, who remain in Costa Rica for more than 30 days are subject to the country's child welfare laws and will not be permitted to leave the country unless both parents request permission from the National Child Welfare Agency or *Patronato Nacional de Infancia* (Calle 19 and Ave. 6). This can pose a real problem for a single parent traveling with kids who overstays the permitted 90 days. One parent or guardian cannot get exit papers without written permission from the non-accompanying other parent. This document must be notarized by a Costa Rican consul in the child's home country.

If you don't adhere to this procedure, your child cannot leave the country. A travel agent or lawyer may be able to get permission from the *Patronato* if given the child's passport and two extra Costa Rican-sized passport photos.

Costa Rica's child protection laws can be a real pain-in-the-neck However, in some cases they can work to your advantage and enable you to stay in the country.

If you support minor children, you cannot be deported from the country under most circumstances. Although we don't recommend using this method, some foreigners remain in the country indefinitely this way. Your attorney can explain how to use this law to protract your stay in the country.

COSTA RICAN CITIZENSHIP

After living in Costa Rica for a number or years many foreigners decide that they want to acquire Costa Rican citizenship. If you can qualify, this is another way to stay in the country legally.

We have been told that after living in Costa Rica for more than 5 years under any of the permanent residency programs, you may apply for citizenship.

Foreign men and women married to a Costa Rican for at least two years who have lived in the country during that period may also become citizens. The only disadvantage is that you may have to relinquish your original citizenship. Costa Rica is the only country in Central America that doesn't accept dual nationality.

As far as we know, the United States does not favor dual nationality for its citizens, but does recognize its existence in some cases. The U.S. Embassy in San José usually does not keep an eye on its citizens who have become naturalized Costa Ricans. Check with the U.S. Embassy in San José for the latest regulations.

We know of a number of North Americans who have both U.S. and Costa Rican citizenship. One expatriate friend uses his Costa Rican passport for travel because he claims there are less problems than with his U.S. passport.

We suggest consulting a Costa Rican attorney for all the details and specific requirements if you are really interested in this subject.

GETTING MARRIED

Getting married in Costa Rica is really quite simple. All you have to do is complete the required paperwork and have the appropriate documents like a passport, divorce papers (if you were previously married), birth certificate and any other pertinent information. We suggest consulting your lawyer if you are marrying in Costa Rica to find out exactly what documents are needed and what procedures to follow.

By the way, lawyers can marry people in Costa Rica much like a justice of the peace in the states. This type of marriage is called *por civil* and is usually quicker than a traditional church wedding or *por la iglesia*. In Costa Rica people get married either way.

If you do choose to have a lawyer marry you, you will need to have two witnesses for the ceremony.

BRINGING AN AUTOMOBILE TO COSTA RICA

Because import taxes on new cars are very high (see Chapter 2) , used cars are plentiful in Costa Rica. Most of these second hand cars are priced higher than they would be in the U.S. or Canada, so Costa Ricans tend to keep them longer and take better care of them. This makes resale value high.

The majority of automobiles in Costa Rica are made in Japan. So, most replacement parts are for Japanese automobiles. Spare parts for U.S. cars have to be imported, are expensive and sometimes hard to come by. Therefore, you should think twice about bringing an Anerican car to Costa Rica. If you do decide to bring a car from the U.S, or Canada it is best to bring a Toyota, Nissan, Honda or some other Japanese import for the reasons just mentioned.

There are two ways to bring a car to Costa Rica—by sea or by land. If you ship your car to Costa Rica by boat, contact a shipping company near to where you have your car in the U.S. or one of the companies mentioned in the next section. This method of transportation is relatively safe since your car can be insured against all possible types of damage.

If you have all of your paperwork in order, your vehicle should not take more than a month to reach Costa Rica depending on your port of embarkation. If you send your car from Miami it only takes two weeks to reach Puerto Limón on the East coast of Costa Rica and costs about $800. From the West coast of New York, you can expect to pay over $1000. One of the advantages of shipping your car is that you can load it with small household goods so you won't have to send them separately. Don't forget to inventory and insure everything. Some cars arrive stripped of their contents. If you have sufficient time and enjoy adventure, drive your automobile to Costa Rica. The journey from the U.S. to Costa Rica (depending on where you cross the Mexican border), takes about three weeks if driving at a moderate speed. (The shortest land distance from the U.S. to Costa Rica is 2250 miles through Brownsville, Texas).

Take your time so you can stop and see some of the sights. We recommend driving only during the day since most roads are poorly lighted if at all. At night large animals—cows, donkeys and horses—can stray onto the road and cause serious accidents.

Your car must be in good mechanical condition before your trip. Carry spare tires and necessary parts. Take a can of gas and try to keep your gas tank as full as possible, because service stations are few and far between.

Have your visas, passports and other necessary papers in order to avoid problems at border crossings. Remember, passports are required for all U.S. citizens driving through Central America. You also need complete car insurance, a valid driver's license and a vehicle registration.

You can buy insurance from AAA in the U.S., or contacting Sanborn's Insurance in the U.S. 512-686-0711. Instant Auto Insurance, offers a 24-hour 800 number and fax service, so you can have you policy ready. In the U.S. and Canada call 1-800-345-47-01 or fax 619-690-65-33. You can also buy insurance at the border before entering Mexico. Having an accident in Mexico is a felony not a misdemeanor. So don't forget to be fully insured.

If you are missing a driver's license, a vehicle registration or insurance, border guards can make your life miserable. Also, remember some border crossings close at night, so plan to arrive at all borders between 8 a.m. and 5 p.m., just to be safe.

When you finally arrive at the Costa Rica-Nicaragua border, expect be delayed clearing customs. If you bring many personal possessions intending to live in Costa Rica permanently, some or all of them may be inventoried and taken to the custom's warehouse in San José. You may pick them up at a later date, after you have paid the necessary taxes.

We understand that a tourist may keep a car in Costa Rica for up to three months. You may apply for a three-month extension which is usually granted, but after six months the vehicle must leave the country or be taxed. Any person who brings a car to Costa Rica and pays all of the taxes, may keep the a car in the country indefinitely as soon as all paperwork is completed.

If you do to keep your vehicle in Costa Rica, here is a simple formula for figure the amount of tax. You pay 100 percent of the value of a new car and 60 percent of the value of a new pickup truck, plus the value of those shipping charges. If the car is a year old, you get a 20% discount. You get a 10% discount for the second, third and fourth years.

For example, on a five year old car you pay taxes on 30% of the value. The value is the manufacturer's suggested retail price. This means if you have a five-year old car that is valued at $9,000 and you paid $1,000 to ship it, you owe the customs $3,000. After 5 years you end up paying about 20% in taxes.

Or take the original value of a vehicle and calculate its depreciation according to the year of the car. For a vehicle from 1990 or before, the value drops 70 percent; 1991, 50 precent; 1992, 40 percent; 1993, 30 percent; 1994, 20 percent. Then add the charge for delivery and insurance (around $600). To this you will have to add a tax on the value of the car, the collective consumer tax, a 1 percent import charge and a sales tax.

However, you may think twice about bringing a used car from abroad. A new tax system about to be introduced will mean increases of up to 100 percent in import taxes, depending on the make and year of car.

After reading the above, if you still decide to import a used vehicle, we recommend using a customs broker to run around and obtain all the necessary documents. However, if you do decide to do this yourself you will need to follow the procedure below.

First, you need to register your car, which takes about ten working days. Then have your vehicle checked at the *Revisión Técnica* at the west end of Sabana Park. Next, take the papers they give you to the *Registro Público* or Public Registry vehicle section (*Registro de Vehículos*). in the suburb of Zapote. Call 506-224-0628 if you need information.

The cost of your registration depends on the value of your car. Finally, take the documents from the registry to the Ministry of Public Works (*Ministerio de Obras Públicas y Transportes*) at Plaza Víquez south of downtown San José. This is the also the place where your license plates will be issued a few months later.

If you want additional information on driving from the U.S. to Costa Rica, you can purchase a new guide book *Driving the Panamerican Highway to Mexico and Central America*, by Raymond and Audrey Pritchard. You can order this book by writing Ray Pritchard, Marketing Consultants, APDO 208-3000, Heredia, Costa Rica, C.A. See the back of this book for details.

SHIPPING YOUR HOUSEHOLD GOODS TO COSTA RICA

As previously stated, the old *pensionado* program allowed retirees to import household items including an automobile virtually duty-free. Since most of these privileges have been rescinded, you may well have second thoughts about importing anything.

Keep in mind that most imported used items are also taxed. Taxes range from 40 to 90 percent or more of the value of the article plus your shipping costs. Taxes can be raised on a whim of the Costa Rican government. Most things you'll want or a similar product is available in Costa Rica, but will cost more than in the U.S., because they are imported. You can, however, save money at the duty-free zone or *depósito libre* in the southern Costa Rican city of Golfito.

The duty-free zone was designed in 1990 for Costa Ricans and residents. Most popular goods sold there are domestic electrical appliances from refrigerators, freezers and stoves to sound systems and television sets. All major brand names are available in a variety of models. Although you may find many of them cheaper in the U.S., they are big bargains compared to San José's prices—up to 50 percent on some large appliances.

Some restrictions and paper work may irk you, but this will be easier for you than importing things from the U.S.

For small items many foreign residents go to the town of David on the Panamanian border. Prices on everything including household goods are nearly as low as in the U.S. However, because of taxes you will have to pay on large electronic goods and appliances, it is better to shop at the duty-free *depósito* across the border in Golfito. Nevertheless, foreign residents living in Costa Rica on a 90-day visa can go to David for 72 hours to renew their papers for another three months.

If you decide to import things and want to save time and money, purchase and ship them from Los Angeles, Houston, New Orleans or preferably Miami. The latter is the U.S. port nearest to Costa Rica and shipping costs are lower. Look in the yellow pages of the Miami phone book for a shipping company or call one of the companies listed below. We understand that some trucking companies will ship your belongings overland.

After taking high shipping costs into consideration, you may be reluctant to ship any household items from the U.S. This is a matter of personal choice. Most foreign residents and even Costa Ricans prefer U.S. products because of their higher quality. However, many retirees live comfortably and happily without luxuries and expensive appliances.

You can rent a furnished apartment. If you choose, you can furnish an apartment, excluding stove and refrigerator, for a few hundred dollars. Wooden furniture is inexpensive in Costa Rica. What you need to import depends on your personal preference and budget.

Here are some money saving tips for bringing your household goods to Costa Rica. First, when entering the country as a tourist by plane, you can bring in a lot of personal effects and small appliances. A tourist is sometimes waved through customs without ever having to open any luggage.

Have friends bring a few things when they come to visit you in Costa Rica. Always try to take as much as possible with you on the plane rather than shipping items by boat, because most used personal things are not taxed at the airport. Even used appliances have a good chance of clearing airport customs if you can fit them on the plane.

Make an effort to get rid of "clutter' and don't ship what can be easily or cheaply replaced in Costa Rica. Talk to other retirees to see what they think is absolutely necessary to bring to Costa Rica.

If you chose to send some of your possessions by ship, you will learn to exercise extreme patience. Be prepared to face many unnecessary delays and frustrations when dealing with the Costa Rican custom's house, or *aduana*.

It is more usual than not to make many trips to the custom's warehouse to get your belongings. You may spend all day going from window to window dealing with mountains of paperwork, only to hear at the end of the day that you must come back tomorrow. Futhermore, fickle customs officials decide the value of the shipped goods and two identical shipments, can be taxed differently, depending who examines them at the *aduana*.

You can ship your belongings in containers or small boxes,

depending on what you have. Used clothing and books are not subject to taxes. So, don't pack them with taxable articles or you may have to pay taxes on them anyway.

Because of this dilatory process, many people pay a local customs broker, *Agencia Aduanera*, or hire some other person or their lawyer to do this unpleasent task for them. It may cost a little more this way, but it will save valuable time. For additional information call or write:

Worldwide Movers Air and Sea Freight
P.O. Box 253-1007
Centro Colón
San José, Costa Rica
Fax 506-233-0517
Tel: 011-506-233-4785
Servex International S.A.
P.O.Box 1285-1000
San José, Costa Rica
Tel: 011-506-53-1152
Fax 506-224-8437

Consult the yellow pages for listing of *Agencias Aduaneras* (Custom's brokers). The Resident's Association suggests you contact moving expert, Carlos Bravo before you decide to ship your belongings to Costa Rica. Tel: 255-1152, Fax; 224-8437.

HOW TO FIND A LAWYER

If you plan to go into business, work, buy or sell property or seek long term residency status in Costa Rica, you will definitely need the services of a good attorney.

Your attorney can help you understand the complexities of the Costa Rican legal system, which is based on Napoleanic law. You are guilty until proven innocent, just the opposite of our system in the U.S.A. A lawyer is one of the best investments you can make because he (or she) can assist you with bureaucratic procedures and handle other legal matters that arise.

If you are not fully bilingual, be sure to choose a lawyer who is. His secretary should be bilingual, too (Spanish/English). This helps avoid communication problems, misunderstandings and enables you to stay on top of your legal affairs.

It is very important to watch your lawyer closely, since most

Costa Rican lawyers tend to drag their feet as bureaucrats do.

Never take anything for granted. Refuse to believe that things are getting done, even if you are assured they are. Check with your lawyer on a regular basis and ask to see your file to make sure he has taken care of business. As you might imagine, paper work moves slowly in Costa Rica, so you don't want a procrastinating lawyer to prolong the process.

When you first contact a lawyer, make sure he is accessible at all hours. Make sure you have your lawyer's office and home telephone number in case you need him in an emergency. If your lawyer is always in meetings or out of the office, this is a clear sign your work is being neglected and you have chosen the wrong lawyer.

Know your lawyer's speciality. Although most attorneys are required to have a general knowledge of Costa Rican law, you may need a specialist to deal with your specific case. Some people find it's a good idea to have several lawyers for precisely this reason.

Take your time and look around when you are trying to find a lawyer. This should be fairly easy since there are over 7,000 lawyers to choose from. You should ask friends, other people, retirees and other knowledgeable people for the names of their lawyers. Then try to inquire about your potential lawyer's reputation and his work methods and integrity.

If you find yourself in a jam before finding a lawyer, contact the Resident's Association for assistance, or you can go to one of the many lawyers' offices near the courthouse.

All over the world, there are always a few incompetent, unscrupulous attorneys, so be careful who you are dealing with before you make your final choice.

Remember, one of the most important people in your life in Costa Rica is your lawyer, so it is imperative that you develop a good working relatonship.

Most attorneys charge from $25 to $50 an hour depending on your problem and their expertise. It is inadvisable to select your lawyer solely on the basis of legal fees. Lawyer's fees, or *honorarios*, vary. Just because a lawyer is expensive doesn't mean he is good. Likewise, you shouldn't select an attorney only because his fees are low.

Check with the Costa Rican version of the Bar Association (*El Colegio de Abogados*) if you have any questions about legal fees.

In Costa Rica it is not uncommon to hire a lawyer on a full-time basis by paying what amounts to a small retainer. If you find a lawyer who will handle your *pensionado* paperwork for under $500 you have found a bargain.

For your information, there is a small amount of paperwork involved in giving your lawyer power of attorney *(poder)* so he can take care of your personal business and legal affairs. This is not a bad idea when you may have to leave the country for a period of time, or in the event of an emergency. However, first make sure your lawyer is completely trustworthy and competent.

If you want answers to most of your questions about the complex Costa Rican legal system, purchase *The Legal Guide To Costa Rica.* Although this book is no substitue for a good lawyer, it is still very useful for the layman.

This comprehensive guide contains sample forms and documents. It covers the most common situations you will encounter in Costa Rica, real estate transactions, corporations, commercial transactions, immigration, labor laws, taxation, wills, marriage and much more. To get a copy write to the address we list in the back of this book.

Here is a partial list of bilingual attorneys who have many North American clients:

Sergio Sánchez Bagnarello
Apdo. 6241-1000
San José, Costa Rica
Tel: 506- 221-6969; Fax: 506-221-5717

Ruhal Barrientos Saborio
Apdo. 5576-1000
San José, Costa Rica
Tel: 506-222-7654; Fax: 506-222-7654

Carballo & Soley
SJO Dept. 201
PO Box 025216
Miami, Fl 33102
or
Apdo. 6997
San José, Costa Rica
Tel: 506-221-031; Fax: 506-223-9151

Henry Lang
Apdo. 10804-1000
San José, Costa Rica
Tel: (506) 221-4536 Fax: 233-1197

COSTA RICAN CONSULATES AND EMBASSIES ABROAD

Anyone seeking permanent residency in Costa Rica needs to have certain documents notarized by a Costa Rican consulate or embassy in their country of origin. Documents that must be notarized are a birth certificate, police certificate (stating you have no criminal record) and a proof of income statement. All this paper work be taken care of before coming to Costa Rica.

If you apply for permanent residency in Costa Rica, it may take months to get notarized documents from your home country if it's possible at all. If worse comes to worst you may even have to make a trip home to take care of these matters. While you are waiting for papers from abroad other documents may expire and you will have to start all over again. Bureaucracy is slow enough as it is in Costa Rica, and it is foolish to delay this process any more than necessary.

Here are some of the Costa Rican Consulates and Embassies abroad:

Consulates in the United States:

Atlanta: 1870 The Exchange N W, #100, Atlanta, GA 30859-2012 Tel: 404-951-7025

Boston: 672 Chesnut Hill, Brookline, MA 02146 Tel: 617-738-9708

Buffalo: 5370 Siegle Road, Lockport, NY 14094

Chicago: 8 S. Michigan Ave., Suite 1312, Chicago, IL 60603

Dallas: 4100 Traris Street, Suite 202, Dallas, TX 75204

Denver: 1633 Filmore Street, Denver, CO 80206; Tel: 303-778-6032; Fax: 303-377-0050

Hawaii: 819 Koto Isle Circle, Honolulu, HI 96825

Houston: 3000 Wilcrest, Suite 145, Houston, TX 77042

Kansas City: 416 W. 61st Street, Kansas City, MO 64113

Las Vegas: P.O. Box 80494, Las Vegas, NV 89180
Tel: 702-363-2925

Los Angeles: 3540 Wilshire Blvd., Suite 404, Los Angeles, CA 90010
Tel: 213-380-7915; FAax: 213-289-1245

Miami: Consulate General, 1600 N.W. Le Jeune Rd., 3rd Floor
Miami, FL 33126 Tel: 305- 871-7485; Fax: 305- 871-0860

New Orleans: Consulate General Costa Rica, 2002 Street 20th,
Suite B-103, Kenner, LA 70062, Tel: 504- 467-1462; Fax: 504-466-8268

New York: 80 S. Wall Street, Suite 1117, New York, NY 10005

Oregon: 14385 S.W. Jenkins Rd. # 126, Beaverton, OR 97005-1158

Orlando: 1213 37th Street, Suite 204 , Orlando, FL 32805
Tel: 407-422-4544; Fax: 407-422-5220

Pittsburgh: 1164 Harvard Road, Monroeville, PA 15146
Tel: 412- 856-7967

Raleigh: 2301 Stonehenge Drive, Suite 2, Raleigh, NC 27015
Tel: 919-676-1422; Fax: 919-676-9734

Salt Lake City: 751 South 300 E., Salt Lake City, UT 84111,
Tel: 801-753-3490/6545

San Antonio: Continental Bldg., 6836 San Pedro, Suite 206B
San Antonio, TX 78216, Tel: 512- 824-8489; Fax: 512-829-5553

San Diego: P.O. Box 880-695, San Diego, CA 92108,
Tel: 619- 277-9447; Fax: 619-563-1059

San Francisco: 870 Market Street, Suite 548, San Francisco, CA 94102
Tel: 415-392-8488; Fax: 415-392-3745

St. Louis: 7700 Bonhomme, Suite 200, Saint Louis, MO 63105
Tel: 314-725-1200; Fax: 314-725-3227

St. Paul: 2400 Kasota Avenue, St. Paul, MN 55108, Tel: 612-645-3401
Fax: 612-645-7444

Vancouver: 8500 N.E. Hazel Dell Ave J-11, Vancouver, WA 98665
Tel: 206-576-0710; Fax: 503-693-0623

Wisconson: 130 Lexington Blvd., White Fish bay, WI 53217, Tel: 414-332-0376

Washington, D.C.: 2114 S Street N.W., Washington, D.C. 20008; Tel: 202-234-2945; Fax: 202- 234-2945

Consulates Abroad:

England
14 Lancaster Gate
London, England
K2P 1B7

Canada
Embassy of Costa Rica
135 York Street, Suite 208
Ottawa, Ontario K1N 5T4
Tel: (613) 562-2855
Fax: (613) 562-2582

Canada
614 Centre A. Street N.W.
Calgary, Alberta

Canada
7 Lia Crescent Don Mills
Toronto, Ontario

Canada
1520 Alberni Street
Vancouver, B.C.

Canada
1155 Dorchester Blvd. W.
Suite 2902, Montreal
P.Q. H3B2L3

EMBASSIES AND CONSULATES IN COSTA RICA

If you are planning to travel and explore Latin America and other parts of the world, when you are settled in Costa Rica, you will need the addresses of the embassies and consulates listed below in order to get visas and other necessary travel documents.

Argentina — Ave. 6 Calle 21-25 221-6869

Austria (consulate) — Ave. 4 Calle 36-38................... 255-0767

Belgium — Los Yoses 225-6255

Belize — Guadalupe 253-9626

Bolivia — Ave. Central, Calle 9-12 233-6244

Brazil — Ave. 2, Calle 20-22 233-1544

Canada — Ave. ct. 1 Calle 3 255-3522

Chile — Barrio Dent 224-4243

China — San Pedro 224-8180

Columbia — Ave. 1, Calle 29 221-0725

Ecuador (consulate) — Paseo Colón, Calle 38-40 226-6282

El Salvador — Los Yoses 225-3861, 224-9034

France — Curridabat 225-0733

Germany — Ave. 5, Calle 40-42 232-5533

Great Britain — Paseo Colón 221-5566

Guatemala —(consulate) Barrio California 233-5283

Honduras — Los Yoses 234-0949, 222-2145

Italy — Los Yoses, Ave. 10, Calle 33-35 234-2326

Israel — Ave., 2-4, Calle 2 221-6011

Jamaica (consulate) — Urb. Los Anonos 228-0802

Japan — Rohrmoser 232-1255

Mexico — Barrio Armon 222-5528, 232-2456

Nicaragua — Barrio California 233-3479

Panamá — San Pedro 225-3401

Paraguay— San Ramón - Tres Rios 233-3794, 225-2802

Perú — Los Yoses 225-9145

Puerto Rico — Ave. 2, Calle 11-13 257-1769

Spain — Ave. 2 (Paseo Colón) Calle 32 222-1933

Switzerland — Paseo Colón, Calle 38-40 233-0052

Taiwan — Guadalupe 224-4992

United States of America — Pavas - Rohrmoser 220-3939

Uruguay — Los Yosas 234-9909, 223-2512

U.S.S.R. — Curridabat 272-1021, 225-5780

Venezuela — Los Yoses 225-5813

CHAPTER NINE

Other Useful
Information

COSTA RICA'S POTABLE WATER

Unlike other countries in Latin America, especially Mexico, Costa Rica's water supply is good and perfectly safe to drink in San José and in the majority of small towns. In most places, you can drink water without fear of  Montezuma's Revenge (dysentery) or other intestinal problems. However, be careful when you drink water in the countryside. We have lived in Costa Rica for years and not heard many people complain about the quality of Costa Rica's water. But if you prefer, bottled water is available. You will be pleased to know that Costa Rica's water is also soft for bathing and washing your hair.

FRUITS, VEGETABLES AND OTHER BARGAIN FOODS

A wide variety of delicious tropical fruits and vegetables grows in Costa Rica. It is amazing that every fruit and vegetable you can think of besides some exotic native varieties flourish there. More common tropical fruits such as pineapples, mangoes and papayas cost about a third of what they do in the United States. Bananas can be purchased at any local fruit stand or street market for about five cents each.

Once you have lived in Costa Rica you can do as many Costa Ricans do and eat a few slices of mouth-watering fruit for breakfast at one of the many sidewalk *fruterías* or fruit stands all over the country. For people living on a tight budget, this healthy fresh fruit breakfast will cost about 50 or 60 cents. There are also many *sodas*, or small cafes, where you can eat a more typical Costa Rican breakfast for around a dollar.

Besides fruits and vegetables, many other bargain foods are available in Costa Rica. Bakeries sell fresh home-made breads and pastries. We recommend the Schmidt chain of bakeries. Other foods such as eggs, chicken, meat, cheese and honey are available at most small neighborhood grocery stores, *pulperías*, as well as large supermarkets. These supermarkets are much like markets in the U.S.; everything is under one roof, but the selection of products is smaller.

Many imported packaged products found in Costa Rican supermarkets are very expensive. It is usual to pay double for your favorite breakfast cereal, certain canned foods or liquor. Don't worry because there are local products to substitute for your favorite U.S. brand. However, if you absolutely cannot live without your foods from the states, you can usually find them at Bubis imported food stores or at the Auto Mercados supermarkets at a very high price. If you want to save money, we suggest you stock-up on these items on shopping trips to the states and bring them back with you by plane. Friends or relatives can bring the food items you need when they visit. If you go to the neighboring country of Panama, you will find many American food products are sold there.

Since most foods are so affordable in Costa Rica, you will be better off changing your eating habits and buying more local products, so you can keep your food bill low. You can save more money by shopping at the Central Market, **Mercado Central**, as many cost-conscious Costa Ricans do. The market covers a whole city block in the heart of downtown San José, near the banking district. Under one roof are hundreds of shops where you can buy fresh fruits, vegetables, grains and much more. You can also go to an open-air street market, called *feria del agricultor*, on any Saturday morning. Farmers bring their fresh produce to these street markets each week, so you can find a variety of produce, meats and eggs at low prices. A few words about Costa Rica's excellent seafood. With oceans on both sides, Costa Rica has a huge variety of fresh seafood. Tuna, dorado, corvina, abound as well as lobster, shrimp of all sizes and some crab. All of these can be purchased at any *pescadería* (fish market) in and around San José's Central Market at low prices. While you're there, try a heaping plate of *ceviche* (fish cocktail) at one of the many fish restaurants called *marisquerías*.

Typical Costa Rican food is similar to that of Mexico and other Central American countries. Tortillas often, but not always, are eaten with a meal of rice, beans, fruit, eggs, vegetables and a little meat. The most common dish, *gallo pinto*, is made with rice and black beans as a base and fried with red bell peppers and cilantro. The best *gallo pinto* is served at La Soda Tapia restaurant opposite Sabana Park in San José.

Some other popular Costa Rican foods include: *casado* the blue-plate special in Spanish (fish, chicken, or meat with beans and chopped cabbage), *empanadas* (a type of stuffed bread turnover), *arreglados* (a kind of sandwich) and *palmito* (heart of palm), which is usually eaten in salads.

MAJOR SUPERMARKETS

PERIFERICOS — several locations in the San José area

MAS POR MENOS — largest chain

AUTO MERCADOS — the best supermarkets in Costa Rica

LA GRAN VIA — downtown San José

BUBIS — specializing in expensive imported food products

PALI SUPERMERCADOS — discount warehouses

CENTRAL MARKET, MERCADO CENTRAL between Avenida Central and 1 and Calle 6 and 8, has great food bargains

RELIGION

Although 90 percent of Costa Ricans are Roman Catholic, there is freedom of religion and other religious views are permitted.

We hope the list of churches we have provided below will help you. Call the number of your denomination to be directed to your nearest house of worship in the San José area. Some churches in the San José area have services in English. (The asterisks denote churches where services in English are held).

```
*   QUAKER ................................................................. 233-6168
    UNITARIAN ............................... 228-1020 or 228-4196
    SYNAGOGUE SHAARE ZION ............................. 222-5449
*   B'NEI ISRAEL .......................................................... 225-8561
    PROTESTANT ........................................................... 228-0553
    UNION CHURCH ...................................................... 226-3670
    MORMON .................................................................. 234-1945
*   YOGA ........................................................................ 221-5895
*   METHODIST ............................................................ 222-0360
*   CHRISTIAN SCIENCE ............................................. 221-0840
    BAPTIST (San Pedro) ............................................. 253-7911
*   EPISCOPAL .............................................................. 222-1560
    ESCAZU CHRISTIAN FELLOWSHIP ....................... 231-5444
    JEHOVAH'S WITNESS .............................................. 221-1436
    SEVENTH DAY ADVENTISTS .................................. 223-7759
    CATHOLIC (Escazú) ................................................ 228-0635
    CATHOLIC (Los Yoses) ........................................... 225-6778
*   CATHOLIC (Rohrmoser) ......................................... 232-2-28
*   CATHOLIC (Barrio San Bosco) .............................. 221-3748
    CATHOLIC (Downtown Cathedral) ........................ 221-3820
    VICTORY CHRISTIAN CENTER ............................. 282-7720
    UNITY CHRIST INTERNATIONAL ......................... 228-6805
```

HOLIDAYS IN COSTA RICA

Costa Ricans are very nationalistic and proudly celebrate their official holidays, called *feriados*. Plan your activities around these  holidays and don't count on getting business of any kind done since most government and private offices will be closed. In fact, the whole country shuts down during *Semana Santa* (the week before Easter) and the week between Christmas and New Year's Day.

January 1	NEW YEAR'S DAY
March 19	SAINT JOSEPH'S DAY
Holy Week	HOLY THURSDAY
	and GOOD FRIDAY
April 11	JUAN SANTA MARIA'S DAY, a local hero
May 1	LABOR DAY
May	UNIVERSITY WEEK
June	FATHER'S DAY, the third Sunday
July 25	ANNEXATION OF GUANACASTE PROVINCE
August 2	VIRGIN OF LOS ANGELES DAY
August 15	MOTHER'S DAY
Saptember 15	INDEPENDENCE DAY
October 12	COLUMBUS DAY - Discovery of America
October 31	HALLOWEEN
November 2	DAY OF THE DEAD
December 8	IMMACULATE CONCEPTION
December 25	CHRISTMAS
December 25t	FERIA DE ZAPOTE (December 25th to January 2nd)
December 25	FIESTAS DEL FIN DEL AÑO

BRINGING YOUR PETS TO COSTA RICA

We did not forget those of you who have pets. There are procedures for bringing your pets into the country that require very little except patience, some paperwork and a small fee.

First, a registered veterinarian from your home town must certify that your pets are free of internal and external parasites. It is necessary that your pet has up-to-date vaccinations against rabies, distemper, leptospirosis, hepatitis and parvovirus and a rabies vaccination within the last three years. Remember, all of these required documents are indispensable and must be certified by the Costa Rican consulate nearest your home town.

If you fail to comply with these regulations and do not provide the required documents, your pet(s) can be refused entry, placed in quarantine or even put to sleep. But don't worry, if worse come to worst, there is a 30-day grace period to straighten things out.

If you want to take your pet out of Costa Rica you will need a special permit, a certificate from a local veterinarian and proof that all vaccinations are up-to-date. When you obtain these documents, take them to the Ministry of Health, and your pet is free to leave the country.

These requirements and additional information and are available from the Departamento de Zoonosis, Ministerio de Salud, Apartado Postal 10123, San José. Telephone 223-0333, extension 331.

VETERINARIANS

Clinica Echandi.. 223-3111
Dr. Federico Piza 248-7166
Dr. Douglas Lutz. 225-6784
Dr. L. Starkey 253-7142
Tecnología Veterinaria (clinic, pharmacy, and boarding) 228-9347
Dr. Lorena Guerra (makes house-calls, also boarding) 228-9887

For additional Veterinarians, look under the heading *"VETERINARIA"* in the yellow pages.

SERVICES FOR THE DISABLED AND HANDICAPPED

Getting around in the U.S. or Canada is hard enough when a person is disabled, but can be even harder in a foreign country.

Handicapped and disabled persons should find living in Costa Rica not much of an obstacle. Some places have wheel chair access. A few hotels like the Grand Hotel Central America, are accessible to the handicapped because they are only one story high. During the rainy season the terrain can sometimes be hard to negociate.

Keep in mind that taxis are inexpensive and the best way to travel for people with physical impediments. Since hired help is such a bargain, a full-time employee may be hired as a companion or as a nurse for a very reasonable price. In addition, medical care is relatively inexpensive in Costa Rica.

There is a social club for disabled veterans that meets once a month. Call 443-9870 for more information.

We suggest that you pick up the book, *Access to the World: A Travel Guide For the Handicapped*, by Louise Weiss, Published by Chatham Square Press, 401 Broadway, New York, NY 10013. This book contains good information and suggestions for disabled travelers.

UNDERSTANDING THE METRIC SYSTEM

If you plan to live in Costa Rica, it is in your best interest to understand the metric system. You will soon notice that automobile speedometers, road mileage signs, the contents of bottles, and rulers are in metric measurements. Since you probably didn't study this system when you were in school and it is almost never used in the U.S., you could become confused.

The conversion guide below will help you.

To Convert:	To:	Multiply by:
Centigrade	Fahrenheit	1.8 then add 32
Square km	Square miles	0.3861
Square km	Acres	247.1
Meters	Yards	1.094
Meters	Feet	3.281
Liters	Pints	2.113
Liters	Gallons	0.2642
Kilometers	Miles	0.6214
Kilograms	Pounds	2.205
Hectares	Acres	2.471
Grams	Ounce	0.03527
Centimeter	Inches	0.3937

* Courtesy of *Costa Rica Today*.

FOR OUR CANADIAN READERS

In order to escape Canada's cold winters, many Canadians live in Costa Rica on a full-or part-time basis. It is therefore not surprising that many businesses and services have been created, catering to Canadians.

Currently there are two separate Canadian clubs helping to make life eaiser for Canadians living or planning to live in Costa Rica. By attending either of these club's meetings people can make new friendships and establish some good contacts. Both organizations provide information about acquiring residency, starting a business, transferring ownership of a car, names of doctors and lawyers and will assist with purchasing medical, automobile and home insurance in Costa Rica. All Canadian visitors and residents are urged to attend. For more information call 438-0043 or 289-6089.

As we mention in Chapter 2, the Canadian-Costa Rican Chamber of Commerce (257-3241) will also be happy to answer questions, if you are thinking of going into business.

The Costa Rican Record is a new magazine dedicated to Costa Rica/ Canadian commerce. This publication is full of ads, investment opportunities and other useful information. They also publish *The Costa Rican Record Guidebook*. This book should be read by any Canadian thinking of doing business or living in Costa Rica.

To obtain either of these publications write: *Costa Rican Record*, SJO 956, P.O. Box 025216, Miami, Fl , USA 33102-5216. Tel/Fax 506-282-7352. There is also a 24-hour information line you may use from Canada 506-257-4466 Ext. 8123.

If you are a Canadian non-resident living in Costa Rica, you should think about receiving the *Canadian Resident Abroad-Update Newsletter*. To get a free subscription, contact Canadian Residents Abroad Inc., 305 Lakeshore Road East, Oakville, Ontario, Canada L6J 1J3. Tel/Fax 905-842-98141.

Please see Chapter 8 for the address of the Canadian embassy in Costa Rica or any of the Costa Rican embassies in Canada if you desire more information.

Finally, additional copies of this book may be purchased in Canada through Milestone Publications. Their address is 3284 Heather Street, Vancouver, B.C. V5Z 3K5, Tel: 604- 875-0611 Fax: 604- 738-5135.

CHAPTER TEN

Parting Thoughts
and Advice

10.

PERSONAL SAFETY IN COSTA RICA

Living in Costa Rica is much safer than residing in most large cities in the United States or Latin American countries, but you should take some precautions insure your own safety.

In Costa Rica the rate for violent crimes is very low, but there is a problem with theft, especially in the larger cities. Thieves tend to look for easy targets, especially foreigners, so you can't be too cautious. Make sure your house or apartment has steel bars on both the windows and garage. The best bars are narrowly spaced, because some thieves use small children as accomplices because they can squeeze through the bars to burglarize your residence.

Make sure your neighborhood has a night watchman if you live in the city. Some male domestic employees are willing to work in this capacity. However, ask for references and closely screen any person you hire. Also, report suspicious people loitering around your premises. Thieves are very patient and often case a residence for a long time to observe your comings and goings. They can and will strike at the most opportune moment for them.

You should take added precautions if you live in a neighborhood where there are many foreigners. Thieves associate foreigners with wealth and look for areas where they cluster together. One possible deterrent, in addition to a night watchman, is to organize a neighborhood watch group in your area. Private home security patrols can provide an alarm system and patrol your area for a monthly fee. If you leave town , get a friend or other trustworthy person to house-sit.

Mountain areas offer some spectacular views and tranquility but are less populated and usually more isolated. This makes them prime targets for burglars and other theives. We have a friend who moved to a beautiful home in the hills, but was burglarized times. Out of desperation he had to hire a watchman and buy guard dogs. Unfortunately, a few weeks later he was robbed while doing an errand in town. This is the down side to living off-the-beaten-path.

If you are really concerned about protecting your valuables, you will be better off living in a condominium complex or an apartment. Both are less susceptible to burglary due to their design and the fact that there is safety in numbers, as the saying goes.

If you own an automobile, you should be especially careful if you have *pensionado* (retiree) license plates. These plates identify you as a foreigner and, in some cases, make you a sitting duck for car burglars who relish breaking into your car and stealing your valuables. Make sure your house or apartment has a garage with iron bars so your car is off the street.

When parking away from your house, always park in parking lots or where there is a watchman. He will look after your car for a few cents an hour when you park it on the street. It is not difficult to find watchmen since they usually approach and offer their services as soon as you park your car.

Pickpockets can be a problem. You should never flaunt your wealth by wearing expensive jewelry or carrying cameras loosely around your neck because they make you an easy mark on the street. It is advisable to find a good way to conceal your money, and never carry it in your back pocket. If you carry large amounts of money, use traveler's checks. Never carry any original documents, such as passports or visas. Make a photocopy of your passport and carry it with you at all times. The authorities will accept most photocopies as a valid form of identification.

Men should also watch out for prostitutes, who are often expert pickpockets and can relieve the unsuspecting of their valuables before they realize it. Men, especially when inebriated or alone, should be careful—or aviod—the"*Gringo* Gulch" area in the vicinity of Morazán

Park, The Holiday Inn and Key Largo Bar. Many muggings have been reported in this area at night.

If you are a single woman living by yourself, never walk alone at night. If you do go out at night, be sure to take a taxi or have a friend go along.

White collar crime exists in Costa Rica and a few dishonest individuals—Americans, Canadians and Costa Ricans included—are always waiting to take your money. We have heard of naive foreigners losing their hard-earned savings to ingenious scams.

On your your first trip to Costa Rica you will probably be besieged by con-men anxious to help you make an investment. Be wary of blue ribbon business deals seemly too good to be true, or any other get-rich quick schemes—non-existant gold mines, fantastic sounding real estate projects, phony high-interest bank investments or property not belonging to the person selling it.

Most people in Costa Rica are honest, hard-working individuals. But don't assume people are honest just because they are nice. Remember it doesn't hurt to be overly cautious.

If you are robbed or swindled under any circumstances, contact the police or the *O.I.J. (Organización de Investigación Judicial)* a special highly efficient investigative unit like the FBI (between Aves. 8 and 10 and Calles 15 and 17 in the middle court house, 255-0122). You may also want to contact the Security Ministry, *Ministerio de Seguridad* at 224-4866. You may not recover your, but you may prevent others from being victimized.

CONCLUSION

Throughout this book we have provided the most up-to-date information available on retirement and living in Costa Rica. We have also provided many useful suggestions to make your life in Costa Rica more enjoyable and help you avoid inconveniences. Adjusting to a new culture can be difficult for some people. Our aim is to make this transition easier, so you can enjoy of all the marvelous things that Costa Rica offers.

Before moving permanently to Costa Rica, we highly recommend spending some time there on a trial basis to see if it is the place for you. We are talking about a couple of months or longer, so you can experience Costa Rican life as it is. Remember visiting Costa Rica as a tourist is quite another thing from living there on a permanent basis. It is also good to visit for extended periods during both the wet and dry seasons, so you have an idea of what the country is like at all times of the year. During your visits, talk to many retirees and gather as much information as possible before making your final decision. It is a good idea to attend one of the Newcomer's Seminars held every Tuesday at the Hotel Irazú except the last Tuesday of each month when they are held at the Hotel Cariari. Besides gathering information, you will learn from other retirees and make some good contacts.

The final step in deciding if you want to make Costa Rica your home, is to try living there for at least a year. That's sufficient time to get an idea of what living in Costa Rica is really like and what problems may confront you while trying to adapt to living in a new culture. It may also let you adjust to the climate and new foods. You can learn all the dos and don'ts, ins and outs and places to go or places to avoid before making your final decision.

You may decide to try seasonal living for a few months a year. Many people spend the summer in the U.S. or Canada and the winter in Costa Rica (which is it's summer), so they can enjoy the best of both worlds—the endless summer. As we mentioned in Chapter 8, it's easy to do, since you can legally stay in the country up to six months as a tourist without having to get any type of permanent residency.

Whether you choose to reside in Costa Rica on a full-or part-time basis, keep in mind the cultural differences and new customs. First, life in Costa Rica is very different. If you expect all things to be exactly as they are in the United States, you are deceiving yourself. The concept of time and punctuality are not important in Latin America. It is not unusual and not considered in bad taste for a person to arrive late for a business appointment or a dinner engagement. This custom can be incomprehensible and infuriating to North Americans, but will not change since it is a deeply rooted tradition.

As we previously mentioned, in most cases bureaucracy moves at a snail's pace in Costa Rica, which can be equally maddening to a foreigner. In addition, the Latin mentality, *machismo*, apparent illogical reasoning, traditions, different laws and ways of doing business, seem incomprehensible to a newcomer.

You will notice countless other different customs and cultural idiosyncrasies after living in Costa Rica for a while. No matter how psychologically secure you are, some culture shock in the new living situation will confront you. The best thing to do is respect the different cultural values, be understanding and patient, and go with the flow. Learning Spanish will easy your way.

Costa Rica is an exciting place to live, but poses many obstacles for the newcomer. Don't expect everything to go smoothly at first or be perfect. By taking the advice we offer throughout this book, and adjusting to the many challenges, you should be able to enjoy all of Costa Rica's wonders.

Our recommendation is—don't burn your bridges or sever your ties with your home country, you may want to return home.

Despite our efforts to update this book constantly, all of the aforementioned data may be subject to change at any given time. So, the authors urge you to be sure to check and see that our information is still accurate.

THANK YOU!

ADDITIONAL RETIREMENT INFORMATION

The *COSTA RICAN OUTLOOK* is an innovative, bi-monthly newsletter with wide ranging coverage that is packed with useful information about Costa Rica and an occasional article about retirement. It also offers insightful retirement trips to Costa Rica a couple of times a year. Reading this newsletter is another good way to keep abreast of events in Costa Rica. You can subscribe for $19.00 a year if you live in the U.S. and $22.00 abroad. Write:

Costa Rican Outlook
P.O. Box 5573
Chula Vista, CA 91912-5573
Tel. 1-800-365-2342; Fax 619- 421-6002

LA VOZ is published by the Costa Rican Resident's Association and not for sale to the general public. If you join the Association, your membership will include a monthly copy of their newsletter. For information:

Costa Rican Resident's Association
Apdo. Postal 700-1011
Y Griega, San José, Costa Rica
Central America.
506- 233-80-68 or 233-1017; Fax 506-222-7862

The **NEWCOMER'S SEMINAR** provides useful information at no charge. These weekly seminars are held each Tuesday at the Hotel Irazú, except on the last Tuesday of every month when they are held at the Hotel Cariari. For information:

The Newcomer's Seminar
Box 962
San José, Costa Rica,
506-232-1355; Fax 506-231-0469

LIFESTYLE EXPLORATIONS has trips for prospective retirees to Costa Rica. To contact them write to:

Lifestyle Explorations
101 Federal Street, Suite 1900
Boston, MA 02110
508-371-4814; Fax 508-369-9192

SUGGESTED READING

BOOKS

The New Key to Costa Rica, by Beatrice Blake. Ulysses Press, Berkeley, California. An excellent, easy to follow guide packed with useful information. We recommend it highly - a must for anyone visiting Costa Rica. The new edition has been expanded to 380 pages.

The Costa Rica Traveler, by Ellen Searby. Windham Bay Press, Box 1198, Occidental CA 95465. This book and *"The New Key to Costa Rica"* are the two best guidebooks for tourists as well as locals. Also a 'must'.

Costa Rica Handbook, by Christopher D. Baker. Moon Publications, P.O. Box 3040, Chico CA 95927-3040. The longest and most extensive guidebook to date.

The Adventure Guide to Costa Rica, by Harry S. Pariser. Hunter Publications, Edison, N.J. 08818. A straight forward easy-to-use guide. Another good guidebook.

***The Essenstial Road Guide for Costa Rica*, by Bill Baker. Apdo. 185-1011 San Jose, Costa Rica. A good guide book if you plan to do a lot of driving in the country. In the U.S. call 1-800-881-8607 or write to International Marketing Partners, Inc., 104 Half Moon Circle, H-3, Hypoluxo, Fl. 33462

*** The Legal Guide to Costa Rica*, by Rodger Peterson. Centro Legal R & M, S.A. Interlink 553, P.O. Box 02-5635, Miami, FL 33152

Costa Rica - A Travel Survival Kit, by Rob Rackowiecki. Lonely Planet Publications, Inc., P.O. 2001A, Berkeley, CA 94702. A good guide book.

Costa Rica, A Natural Destination, by Ree Strange Sheck. John Muir Publications, Santa Fe, NM. This book deals mostly with Costa Rica's natural wonders and ecology. Great for nature lovers.

The Costa Ricans, by Richard, Karen, and Mavis Biesanz. Waveland Press, Prospect Heights, IL.

Living in Costa Rica, by the U. S. Mission Association. Loaded with excellent information, and a good reference book.

How You Can Avoid Losses Buying Costa Rican Real Estate*, by Bill Baker, 104 Half Moon Circle H-3, Hypoluxo, Fl. 33462. Another excellent publication by Mr. Baker deals with the real estate market in Costa Rica and helps the reader develop a plan for investing.

Costa Rica, by Harvey Haber. Houghton Mifflin, 2 Park St., Boston, Mass 02108. Beautiful full-color guidebook.

Costa Rica, by Paul Glassman. Passport Press, Box 1346, Champlain, NY, 12919. A good guide with many maps.

Exploring Costa Rica, The Tico Times 1994-1995 Guide*. This 264-page book is available through the *Tico Times* and our company, Costa Rica Books. With its wealth of information about Costa Rica, it is an excellent resource book.

Driving the Panamerican Highway to Mexico and Central America*, by Raymond & Audrey Pritchard. Marketing Consultants, Apdo. 208-3000, Heridia, Costa Rica. This is the only book available if you are planning to drive from the U.S. to Costa Rica via the Panamerican highway. Also available from our company Costa Rica Books.

Developing and Managing Profitable Rental Real Estate in Costa Rica*, Frank J. Thomas Gallardo. Editorial Texto, SJO 1065, P.O. Box 025216, Miami, FL 33102-5216.

Adventures Abroad, Exploring the Travel/Retirement Option, by Allene Symons and Jane Parker. Gateway Books, San Rafael, Ca, 1991. Good retirement tips for many countries including Costa Rica.

Purchasing Real Estate in Costa Rica, by Attorney Alvaro Carballo. Apartado 6997-1000, San José, Costa Rica. FAX 506-223-9151. This guide clears up a lot of misinformation and eases the anxiety of purchasing real estate in a foreign country.

Mexico and Central America Handbook, distributed by Rand McNally. Not as detailed as books that deal specifically with Costa Rica.

Frommer's Costa Rica, Guatemala and Belize on $35 a Day, published by Prentice-Hall Press, 1991. A good guide book for travelers.

SUGGESTED READING

Medical Systems of Costa Rica, by Frank Chalfont. Dept. 257-SJO, P.O. Box 025216, Miami, FL 33102-5216.

Insurance in Costa Rica, by David R. Garrett. Garrett and Asosiados, SJO 450, P.O. Box 025216, Miami, FL 33102-5216.

PERIODICALS

Costa Rica Today newspaper, published weekly. See page 62 for subscription details. This newspaper is more for tourists than the *Tico Times*, more colorful and pleasing to the eye.

The Tico Times newspaper, published weekly. See page 62 for subscription details. Not as upbeat as the competition, *Costa Rica Today*, but definitely worth subscribing to if you are interested in living in Costa Rica.

Adventures in Costa Rica is a newly published newsletter filled with useful information. Contact Starflame Publications, P.O. Box 508, Jackson, CA 95642. 209-223-2771, or 296-5109; FAX 209-223-1588.

The Reach-Out Telephone Directory, co-sponsored by the Tico Times and AT&T. Ossuli, S.A., Apartado 6426-1000, San José, Costa Rica. Lists services (doctors, taxis, dentists, etc.) in Costa Rica where English is spoken.

Costa Rica Outdoors, is a newly published newsletter that covers almost all of the country's outdoor activities. To subscribe write to: Costa Rica Outdoors, Dept. SJO 2316, P.O. Box 025216, Miami, FL 33102-5216. You can also call or fax 011-506-282-6743.

VIDEOS

Living, Retiring and Investing in Costa Rica, is the best video available if you plan to live or invest in Costa Rica. It is the perfect compliment to our book. Write: Odyssey 1 Video Productions, 1016-1 Morraine Way, Green Bay, WI 54303 or call 414-494-1582.

*** All of the titles above with a double asterisk **, are also available through Costa Rica Books' mail order catalog: P.O. Box 1512, Thousand Oaks, CA, 91358. Write for details and a complete price list.

IMPORTANT SPANISH PHRASES AND VOCABULARY

You should know all of the vocabulary below if you plan to live in Costa Rica.

What's your name?	*¿ Cómo se llama usted?*
Hello!	*¡Hola!*
Good Morning	*Buenos días*
Good Afternoon	*Buenas tardes*
Good night	*Buenas noches*
How much is it?	*¿Cuánto es?*
How much is it worth?	*¿Cuánto vale?*
I like	*Me gusta*
You like	*Le gusta*
Where is...?	*¿Dónde está...?*
Help!	*¡Socorro!*

What's the rate of exchange
¿Cuál es el tipo de cambio?

I'm sick	*Estoy enfermo*

where	*dónde*
what	*qué*
when	*cuándo*
how much	*cuánto*
how	*cómo*
which	*cuál or cuáles*
why	*por qué*
now	*ahora*
later	*más tarde*
tomorrow	*mañana*
tonight	*esta noche*

yesterday	*ayer*
day before yesterday	*anteayer*
day after tomorrow	*pasado mañana*
week	*la semana*
Sunday	*domingo*
Monday	*lunes*
Tuesday	*martes*
Wednesday	*miércoles*
Thursday	*jueues*
Friday	*vienes*
Saturday	*sábado*
month	*mes*
January	*enero*
February	*febrero*

IMPORTANT VOCABULARY

March	*marzo*		fat	*gordo*
April	*abril*		thin	*delgado*
May	*mayo*		tall	*alto*
June	*junio*		short	*bajo*
July	*julio*		tired	*cansado*
August	*agosto*		bored	*aburrido*
September	*septiembre*		happy	*contento*
October	*octubre*		sad	*triste*
November	*noviembre*			
December	*diciembre*		expensive	*caro*
			cheap	*barato*
spring	*primavera*		more	*más*
summer	*verano*		less	*menos*
fall	*otoño*		inside	*adentro*
winter	*invierno*		outside	*afuera*
			good	*bueno*
north	*norte*		bad	*malo*
south	*sur*		slow	*lento*
east	*este*		fast	*rápido*
west	*oeste*		right	*correcto*
			wrong	*equivocado*
left	*izquierda*		full	*lleno*
right	*derecha*		empty	*vacío*
easy	*fácil*		early	*temprano*
difficult	*difícil*		late	*tarde*
big	*grande*		best	*el mejor*
small	*pequeño, chiquito*		worst	*el peor*
a lot	*mucho*		I understand	*comprendo*
a little	*poco*		I don't	
there	*allí*		understand	*no comprendo*
here	*aquí*		Do you speak	
nice, pretty	*bonito*		English?	*¿Habla usted inglés?*
ugly	*feo*			
old	*viejo*		hurry up!	*¡apúrese!*
young	*joven*		O.K.	*está bien*

excuse me!	*¡perdón!*	post office	*el correo*	
Watch out!	*¡cuidado!*	passport	*pasaporte*	
		waiter	*el salonero*	
open	*abierto*	bill	*la cuenta*	
closed	*cerrado*			
occupied		blue	*azul*	
(in use)	*ocupado*	green	*verde*	
free (no cost)	*gratis*	black	*negro*	
against the		white	*blanco*	
rules or law	*prohibido*	red	*rojo*	
exit	*la salida*	yellow	*amarillo*	
entrance	*la entrada*	pink	*rosado*	
stop	*alto*	orange	*anaranjado*	
		brown	*café, castaño*	
breakfast	*el desayuno*	purple	*morado,*	
lunch	*el almuerzo*		*púrpura*	
dinner	*la cena*			
cabin	*la cabina*	0	*cero*	
bag	*la bolsa*	1	*uno*	
sugar	*el azúcar*	2	*dos*	
water	*el agua*	3	*trés*	
coffee	*el café*	4	*cuatro*	
street	*la calle*	5	*cinco*	
avenue	*la avenida*	6	*seis*	
beer	*la cerveza*	7	*siete*	
market	*el mercado*	8	*ocho*	
ranch	*la finca*	9	*nueve*	
doctor	*el médico*	10	*diez*	
egg	*el huevo*	11	*once*	
bread	*el pan*	12	*doce*	
meat	*el carne*	13	*trece*	
milk	*la leche*	14	*catorce*	
fish	*el pescado*	15	*quince*	
ice cream	*el helado*	16	*diez y seis*	
salt	*la sal*	17	*diez y siete*	
pepper	*la pimienta*	18	*diez y ocho*	

40	cuarenta	400	cuatrocientos
50	cincuenta	500	quinientos
60	sesenta	600	seiscientos
70	setenta	700	setecientos
80	ochenta	800	ochocientos
90	noventa	900	novecientos
100	cien	1000	mil
200	doscientos	1,000,000	un millón
300	trescientos		

* If you want to perfect your Spanish, we suggest you purchase our best-selling Spanish book, *"The Costa Rican Spanish Survival Course"*, and 90-minute cassette mentioned in Chapter 3. It is a one-of-a-kind pocket-sized course designed for people who want to learn to speak Spanish the Costa Rican way.

TIQUISMOS

Here are some Costa Rican expressions you should be familiar with if you plan to spend a lot of time in Costa Rica.

birra	beer	*maje*	pal
¡Bueno Nota!	Fantastic! Great!	*pachanga*	party
campo	space (on a bus)	*paja*	B.S.
chapa	a coin or stupid person	*pinche*	a tightfisted person
chicha	anger	*pulpería*	corner grocery store
chunche	a thing	*queque*	cake
dar pelota	flirt	*roco*	old person
fila	line	*¡Salado!*	Too bad! Tough luck!
gato	blue-eyed person	*soda*	a small cafe*Tico*
goma	hangover	*Tico*	a Costa Rican
harina	money	*timba*	big stomach
jalar una torta	get in trouble	*tiquicia*	Costa Rica
¡Jale!	Hurry up!	*vino*	snoopy person
macho	blond person	*vos*	you, informal equivalent of tú

MORE PHONE NUMBERS

ACCOUNTANTS

FINWELL, GORDON 2241351

HOUSEMAN, DAVID .... 223-2787 or 239-2045

BANKS

BANCO CREDITO AGRICOLA DE CARTAGO 251-3011

BANCO DE COSTA RICA 255-1100

BANCO NACIONAL DE COSTA RICA 223-2166

BANCO BANEX (PRIVATE) 221-6344

BANCO LYON (PRIVATE) 221-2212

BOTTLED WATER

DE LA MONTANA. 220-0616

BUSINESS AND SECRETARIAL SERVICES

BILINGUAL SECRETARIAL SERVICES 228-4367

CAR PARTS

REPUESTOS CHINO 233-1190

CAR RENTALS

AVIS RENT-A-CAR. 232-9922

BUDGET 223-3284

HERTZ 221-1818

JEEPS "R" US 289-9920

RENT- A -ROVER 33-3037/225-3948

CREDIT CARD COMPANIES

AMERICAN EXPRESS 233-0044

DINNERS CLUB 233-0455

VISA 223-2211

CUSTOMS AGENTS

ADUMAR 223-2233

AGENCIA ADUANAL, S.A. 2231122

APA MOVERS 233-4785

DENTISTS

ACOSTA, AURTURO 228-9904

DEPASS, RONALD 228-9933

HIRSCH, RONALD (CHILDREN'S DENTIST) 222-1081

PISZK, WALTER 222-0363

DOCTORS

AGGERO, ROLANDO 255-4476

ARCE, LUIS R. (EAR, NOSE AND THROAT) 235-5653

ARELLANO, ALFONSO (CARDIOLOGIST) 233-5435

BOLANOS, PEDRO (ORTHOPEDIIC SURGEON) 231-3165

ESQUIVEL, JULIO (GYNAECOLOGY) 220-1010

GABRIEL,PATRICK (CHIROPRACTOR) 296-0020

KOGEL, STEVEN (AMERICAN PSYCHIATRIST). . 253-4502 or 225-7149

LABORATORY LABIN 222-1987

MURRAY, CHARLES (PSYCHOLOGICAL COUNSELING) 260-9902

NUNEZ, RODOLPHP (DERMATOLOGY) 222-6265

PARDO, ROGELIO (INTERNAL MEDICINE) 222-1010

RUBINSTEIN, BERNARDO (OPHTHALMOLOGIST) 221-7709

INSURANCE AGENTS

GARRETT Y ASOCIADOS 233-2455

INTERPRETERS AND TRANSLATORS

TEMPO, S.A. 222-7844

LAUNDRY

LAVA Y SECA 224-5098

SOL Y FIESTA LAVA ROPA. 257-7151

ROBERT .... Plaza Colonial, San Rafael de Escazú

MAILING SERVICES (PRIVATE)

AEROCASILLAS 255--4567

TRANS-EXPRESS INTERLINK 232-2544

AAA EXPRESS MAIL 233-4993

STAR BOX 221-9092

REAL ESTATE

AMERICAN REALITY 223-0328

CARICO 233-8057

CORONADO REALTY 221-3174

FIND-A-HOME 233-5215

RICH COAST REALTY .... TEL: 231-5007 FAX: 296-2738

TAXIS

AEROPUERTO.. 241-0333

COOPEIRAZU 254-3211

COOPETAXI... 235-9966

COOPEUNO.. 254-6768

TAXI ALFARO 221-8466

TAXI COOPEGUARIA 226-1366

TAXIS DE CARGA Y MUDANZAS (FOR MOVING) 223-0921

TRAVEL AGENCIES

SWISS TRAVEL S.A. .... 222-4622, 239-0467 or 232-5362

VIATUR.................................... 225-2355 or 257-1466

INDEX

NOTES

NOTES

NOTES

NOTES

NOTES

NOTES